BC

F 394 .E5 M36
Mangan, Frank J.
El Paso in pictures

D0929508

Southern Pacific Railroad Station in El Paso; 1884. (From the map of "Satterthwaite's Addition to El Paso, Texas")

el paso

IN PICTURES

FOR CHARLES DENT
WITH WARM REGARDS
AND HOPES THAT YOU
ENJOY THE SOUTHWEST
AND EL PASO

FRANK MANGAN

el paso
IN PICTURES

Text and design by

FRANK MANGAN

1971: The Press/El Paso

El Paso, Texas

F
344
. E94
M36

COPYRIGHT 1971
FRANK MANGAN
First Printing 1971
Second Printing 1972
Third Printing 1974
Fourth Printing 1979
Library of Congress Catalog Card No. 70-184833
ISBN 0-930208-02-1

to the photographers
of my favorite town
whose pictures made
this book possible.

CONTENTS

JUAN DE OÑATE arrived at
the Pass in 1598 to take
formal possession of the land for the
King of Spain. Oñate's wife was
the daughter of Cortez, the
conqueror of Mexico, and the
great-granddaughter of Montezuma.

one

They came to the Pass of the North

THE mountain looms up out of the sand-hills, a lonely sentinel in an empty desert. This bare spine of a mountain gazes down at the gorge where a river churns deep and green as it cuts its way through the pass, then widens into the valley below. Tall grass and cattails reach up from the river's meandering banks to the cottonwood trees that line the water's edge. The wild grass and chamizo weeds near the river give way to sandhills and a mesquite-studded plain that slopes gradually upward to the mountain's base, little more than a mile away.

The only movement is that of a hawk, hanging lazily in the sky. There are no human beings, no sounds, except the wind rustling through the cottonwoods. Just empty space and sunshine and blue sky and the mountain that sits like a lonely ship anchored in this sea of grass and desert sand.

The year was 1536 and into this empty landscape wandered an incredible man named Alvar Nuñez Cabeza de Vaca, conquistador. DeVaca, gaunt and sunburned and nearly naked, was accompanied by two Spanish companions and a Moorish servant when he reached the pass of the Rio Grande. He was afoot and he wore no gleaming armor. He was lucky to be alive. He and his little band were sole survivors of an ill-fated Spanish expedition that had set out to conquer Florida six years earlier. The fury of a storm in the Gulf of Mexico cast them ashore on the Texas coast, and they had walked slowly westward until they came to rest that day in 1536. They found an oasis on the park-like banks of the river in the shadow of the mountain that was one day to become known as Mt. Franklin.

After a brief rest, Cabeza de Vaca made his way back southward to Culiacan and the civilized outposts of New Spain on the west coast, carrying with him the distinction of being the first European to set foot on the Pass of the North.

EVEN in 1536, however, these hardy Spaniards were rank newcomers to the river crossing. It had always been a natural stopping place for travelers moving in any direction. The migrations of North American Indian tribes moving southward into Mexico and South America went through this pass. Ten thousand years before, Folsom Man had left his imprint when he came here following the great herds of super bison migrating from the plains into this river valley. Even today, archaeologists continue to turn up the uniquely-designed Folsom arrow points that tell the story of early man's bison hunting adventures in the El Paso area.

But the arrival of the first Spaniards turned out to be more than just another routine river crossing. Back in Mexico, the stories told by Cabeza de Vaca and his companions created a northward movement of Spanish conquistadors.

They moved in and ruled the area with a heavy hand, and for almost three hundred years the flag of Spain waved briskly at the Pass.

As Spain's influence spread northward, the Pass became a natural stopover for wagon trains, young men in search of adventure, and expeditions authorized by the Spanish Crown to keep a firm hold on its northern frontier. As early as 1659, Spanish padres, supervising the local Indian tribes, began building a mission on the south bank of the river. They called it Nuestra Señora de Guadalupe, and the original building, in what is now Juarez, is still standing and in daily use today.

THE hand of Spain remained firm until 1821, when Mexico won its fight for independence and things at the Pass came under new management. Six years later an enterprising Mexican named Juan Maria Ponce de Leon built the first house on the north bank of the Rio Grande — about where the White House Department Store is now located. After applying to the Chihuahua government for a land grant, he received title to about 500 acres on the north side of the river, and all of what later became downtown El Paso cost him only eighty dollars.

After the Mexican War Ponce sold his ranch to an American trader named Benjamin Franklin Coons and the area began to take on the appearance of a little town. It even had a name: Franklin, Texas. The town — such as it was — grew slowly; pretty much as a stopover for travelers going to Chihuahua or Santa Fe. In 1849, the first American troops arrived and established a post to help protect this part of the frontier from marauding Apaches. The military has been a part of the El Paso scene almost constantly since then. Meanwhile, emigrant trains from the East started westward toward California, and they found the friendly oasis of El Paso a pleasant stopover point. It was the only year-around snow-free route West. In 1850, the cattle drives to California began as the new California residents seeking easy gold, created a demand for beef which Texas ranchers were eager to satisfy. Thousands of head of longhorn cattle trailed through and crossed the Rio Grande at El Paso during the next few years. Most travelers stayed only long enough to rest a day or so, drink some El Paso wine, buy provisions, and take another crack at the desert.

By this time the El Paso area included the holdings of a few other Anglo-Americans, the rambling adobe home of Santa Fe trader James Magoffin, and the ranch of Hugh Stephenson, a mountain man and also a Santa Fe trader. Simeon Hart built a flour mill on the rapids of the Rio Grande at the site of what is now the Hacienda Restaurant.

Since the international boundary between Texas and Chihuahua was somewhat fuzzy in those first years after the Mexican War, both countries decided to remedy the situation. In 1850, the United States International Boundary Commission arrived in El Paso to join the Mexican commission in surveying the boundary. John Bartlett headed the American commission and the description in his diary of El Paso in 1852 vividly portrays the frontier as it was at mid-century:

"The town of El Paso del Norte is on the Mexican side of the river. On the American side there was no settlement until after the war . . . At present there are three settlements here, viz., Mr. Coons' ranch with its adjoining buildings, which was formerly the military post; Mr. Stephenson's ranch with another group of buildings; and Magoffinsville. This last is now the principal settlement and represents the American El Paso. It consists of a large square, around which are substantial adobe buildings of a better description than usual embracing some six or eight large stores and warehouses, well-filled with merchandise. This town is admirably situated and belongs wholly to James W. Magoffin, Esq., an American, long resident in Mexico whose energy and public spirit will undoubtedly make it a principal place on the frontier."

MINTED in Mexico City, silver eight real pieces like this circulated in the 1700's around El Paso. These were the "pieces of eight" of pirate lore—called Dos Mundos (two worlds) dollars, the design signifying the old and new worlds with the crown of Spain on top, the conquered seas below. For ease in spending, coins of this design were sliced into segments called "bits". From these came the American terms "two bits" and "four bits". Eight of these segments were worth a dollar.

BARTLETT also reported less prosaic activities such as Indian raids: "The Apaches had been more bold than usual during the spring and summer of 1852. At Frontera, a man was pierced with arrows while herding the animals within a few rods of the house. On two occasions, while I remained at Magoffinsville, the Indians made attempts to run off the animals of the Commission . . . no one could venture alone, with safety, three miles from the settlement and when I went to take a ride, if it was extended as far as three miles, I felt it necessary to be accompanied by several friends. Such was the state of the Mexican frontier in 1852."

But real progress was right around the corner. Two years later the Jackass Mail, the first mail stage from the East and West coasts, clippety-clopped through El Paso. In 1858, the Butterfield Overland Mail made its first run from Tipton, Missouri, through El Paso and on to San Francisco. El Paso became a division point for the Butterfield stagecoaches, and business was so good the company built El Paso's first two-

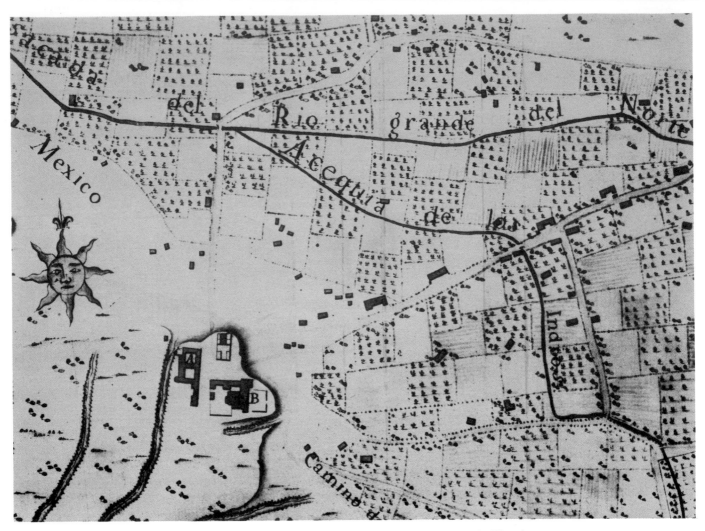

SPANISH MAP of Juarez was made in 1766 by an engineer named Joseph de Urrutia who mapped a number of Spain's northern provinces on orders from the Viceroy in Mexico City. This map, owned by the British Museum, shows the Juarez Mission (marked B) and the garrison for a small detachment of Spanish soldiers (marked A). Nearby are orchards and fields watered by irrigation ditches from the Rio Grande. The faint beginnings of 16th of September Street can be seen running to the northeast from the map's center.

story building. The bright red and canary yellow coaches traveled a route so well designed that in later years, when highway engineers first built the El Paso-Carlsbad highway, they followed closely the original route of the Butterfield. Even today, Interstate 10 west of El Paso parallels the Butterfield route. Highway drivers are either on or in sight of the old trail as they speed across the Southwest in air-conditioned comfort.

MEANWHILE, El Paso continued to be known as Franklin until 1859 when Anson Mills surveyed the townsite and made an approved map showing each block in town. A real estate company was formed to sell lots, and at this point in history, El Paso finally took on the appearance of a "real" town. The 1860 census listed 428 residents. A year later, the Civil War broke out and the garrison at Fort Bliss was ordered to surrender to the Confederacy. This order included all other Texas army posts as well.

Fort Bliss served for a time as headquarters for Confederate activity in the area, but in little more than a year, Union troops arrived from the West and occupied Fort Bliss once again. The Confederates in El Paso were cut off and forgotten for the rest of the war.

In 1873, El Paso became an incorporated town, and Ben Dowell, a saloon keeper, was elected as the first mayor. Life on the frontier went on as usual, but a feeling of progress and prosperity was in the air as El Pasoans began to dream about the coming of the railroads.

The first arrivals

At least ten thousand years ago the great granddaddy of the American Indian, Folsom Man, roamed what is now the city of El Paso. He was a big-game hunter following the migrations of the animals. But other than a few of his flint tools and weapons, he didn't leave us much. He evolved slowly over the centuries — up until 900 A.D. — into what the archaeologists call the Desert Culture. His numbers were sparse, but he was able to eke out a living off the land, eating mesquite pods, mescal cactus, and small game animals.

About 900 A.D., the local El Pasoan became a farmer. He raised corn in the moist land along the river's edge and he lived in small villages of pit houses built below the surface of the ground. Then about 1250 A.D. he entered a transitional phase (which has not yet been given an official name). He moved to the surface, and he built adobe pueblos of up to forty rooms. In those days there was much more rainfall than there is today. In what is now northeast El Paso there were a number of good-sized lakes, and pueblos were scattered all through the area. They lived pretty well with this abundant water supply. El Paso archaeologists have unearthed some splendid examples of pottery from northern New Mexico as well as from Casas Grandes in Chihuahua, proving that the El Paso of the 1300's also had tourists.

When the Spaniards arrived in this part of their empire they were met by the Suma and Manso Indians. There has never been Spanish mention of any permanent Indian settlement at El Paso, but by the time the Spaniards arrived the environment was changing, and a dry cycle began which continues to this day. A tribe called the Piros came to the Pass about the time the Spanish were building the Guadalupe Mission in 1659.

The Indians of New Mexico revolted in 1680, killing many of the Spanish priests and settlers.

IN NORTHEAST EL PASO, Indians used this twenty-inch-high pottery bowl sometime between 1150 and 1400 when large lakes dotted the area. This bowl, called El Paso Polychrome by archaeologists, is on display at UTEP's El Paso Centennial Museum.

Many survivors fled south to El Paso, and with them came some three hundred Christian Indians from the New Mexico pueblos of Isleta and Socorro. They formed the nucleus of the new towns of Ysleta and Socorro a few miles down the river from El Paso and established two missions which were to be the first ever built in Texas. A presidio chapel, San Elizario, was founded in 1773 about fifty miles south of El Paso. In the 1780's it was moved to its present location in the El Paso valley. All of these are still in daily use. The Tigua Indian tribe settled in Ysleta, and its descendants still hold Tigua ceremonials in an Indian-Christian form.

In the 1680's there was little mention of the Apaches. But after 1700, a series of epidemics swept like grass fires through New Spain, wiping out many of the Sumas and most of the Mansos around El Paso. It was then that the Apaches moved in to make themselves known and feared on the frontier. The highly mobile Apaches never really settled at the Pass; they merely raided and dissolved into the inaccessible mountains. The Southwest Indian wars came to an end in 1886 when Geronimo surrendered to General Crook in Mexico.

THE FIRST EUROPEAN to set foot in what is now El Paso was an incredible man named Cabeza de Vaca. In 1536 he and several companions wandered into the Pass after being shipwrecked on the Texas coast.

In 1692, the warrior deVargas recaptured Santa Fe after the Indian revolt.

Outpost of New Spain

It was almost half a century after Cabeza de Vaca and his wanderers crossed the Pass in 1536 that the next Spaniards came this way. In 1581, the Franciscan friar Augustin Rodriguez led a small party up the Rio Grande on a journey to convert Indians in northern New Mexico. The Franciscans were murdered within a few months by the Indians.

Next to come to this Spanish outpost was Don Antonio de Espejo, a great explorer whose assignment was to go to the aid of the missionaries. He came through the Pass in 1582, and within a year he had roamed from the Hopi villages in the west to the prairies east of the Pecos. The success of his journey was a big step in the Spanish colonization of the Southwest.

The man who gave El Paso its name was Juan de Oñate, a colorful conquistador who officially took possession of the new domain in 1598, al-most a quarter century before the pilgrim fathers landed at Plymouth Rock. Late in April that year a large force of soldiers and colonists reached the Rio Grande somewhere near Socorro and then proceeded up river to the crossing at El Paso. Oñate officially named it El Paso del Rio del Norte. In time, Oñate was the one who accomplished the successful colonization of New Mexico.

After the Indians of New Mexico revolted in 1680 and drove the Spanish out of the province —to the safe refuge of El Paso—a re-conquest of New Mexico took place in 1692 under the leadership of Diego de Vargas. The warrior de Vargas with a force of less than three hundred men marched up the Rio Grande and captured the town of Santa Fe. De Vargas subdued the Indians so effectively that New Mexico remained peaceful for more than a hundred years.

Diego de Vargas Zapata Lujan Ponce de Leon

Almost a quarter-century before the Pilgrims landed on Plymouth Rock, Juan de Onate gave El Paso its name— El Paso del Rio Del Norte.

EARLY EXPLORERS in the Southwest wore medieval helmets like this one owned by UTEP's El Paso Centennial Museum. This style was used in Onate's time, until about 1600.

THE JUAREZ MISSION, Nuestra Señora de Guadalupe was founded in 1659. This drawing shows the mission as it looked about two hundred years after its founding.

FORT BLISS was located at Magoffinsville in 1857. Note Mt. Franklin at left in this engraving made at the time. This location can be seen today at the corner of Magoffin Avenue and Willow Street.

Frontier fort

When a major named Jefferson Van Horne arrived in El Paso at the head of a column of troops in 1849 his mission was to establish a military outpost at El Paso to protect travelers, pioneers and settlers from hostile and marauding Indians. The mission also called for building a wagon road across the territory for emigrants using the southern route to California, and to acquire knowledge of the immense, little-known land which surrounded El Paso. He built the first post, and in 1854, it was officially named Fort Bliss in honor of Brevet Lieutenant Colonel William W. S. Bliss who was Zachary Taylor's adjutant general in the Mexican War. In the 1850's, even as today, the social life of the Fort was closely tied to that of El Paso. Bliss was a highly desirable post at which to be stationed. There were always plenty of parties and dances, with both civilian and military guests attending.

The settlers saw the soldiers as protection against the Indians, and the soldiers found the civilians a relief from their loneliness. This friendliness between the military and civilian communities that began more than a hundred years ago continues even today in the close cooperation between city and post.

BACHELOR'S HALL at Fort Bliss in 1860. The old frontier post
which once protected the border from Indian and bandit raids is today
the largest air defense center in the free world.

THE CAMEL CARAVAN
surprised El Pasoans when it came
through on its way from the Texas
Gulf Coast to California in 1857.
The Army decided to experiment
with imported camels as
substitutes for mules on the Southwestern deserts. The experiment
was not an overwhelming success
and the camels were turned loose to
forage for themselves. In time they
multiplied and for years were seen
wandering wild by prospectors and
emigrants.

THIS CLASSIC PHOTO is the oldest known of El Paso Street looking south from Pioneer Plaza. It was taken in 1880 and shows the large cottonwood trees growing on the banks of the acequia (irrigation canal) which flowed down San Francisco Street at right. At left is the famous "newspaper tree" which was used to post notices. The sign on the center tree reads "Conklin's Real Estate Agency," possibly the first one in business in El Paso.

EARLY EL PASOANS pose for their picture outside the Central Hotel. This photograph was taken about 1870 and may be the first ever made in El Paso. At right is the home of Ponce de Leon, El Paso's first settler. This is now the location of the White House Department Store and Mills Building.

IN 1880, people crossed the Rio Grande by wading, swimming, riding or being ferried across by rowboat. This ferry operated at the foot of El Paso Street, and the boatman pulled his passengers across by a stout rope stretched across the river.

In 1859 Anson Mills' map showed each block in town

ANSON MILLS received ownership to a number of lots in downtown El Paso for his work in surveying the townsite and making this map. The Butterfield Overland Mail had arrived in El Paso and made it a division point in 1858 (St. Louis to San Francisco). With this in mind, the map artist drew in the little stagecoaches heading west on San Francisco Street, east on St. Louis Street, and southeast on San Antonio Street. Note also the El Paso acequia that brought irrigation water from the Rio Grande along San Francisco Street. The canal cut directly across the plaza in front of what is now the Mills Building, following an easterly course through town and running across what is now the tower of the State National Bank Building.

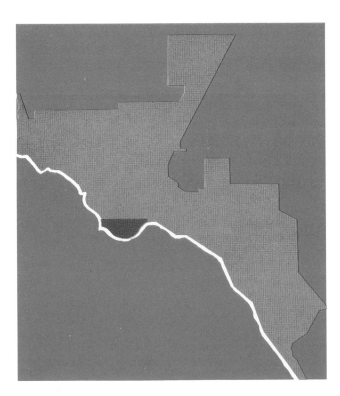

CITY LIMITS in 1873 (dark color) is shown in relation to 1971 city limits (light gray). By 1889 El Paso had only seven square miles.

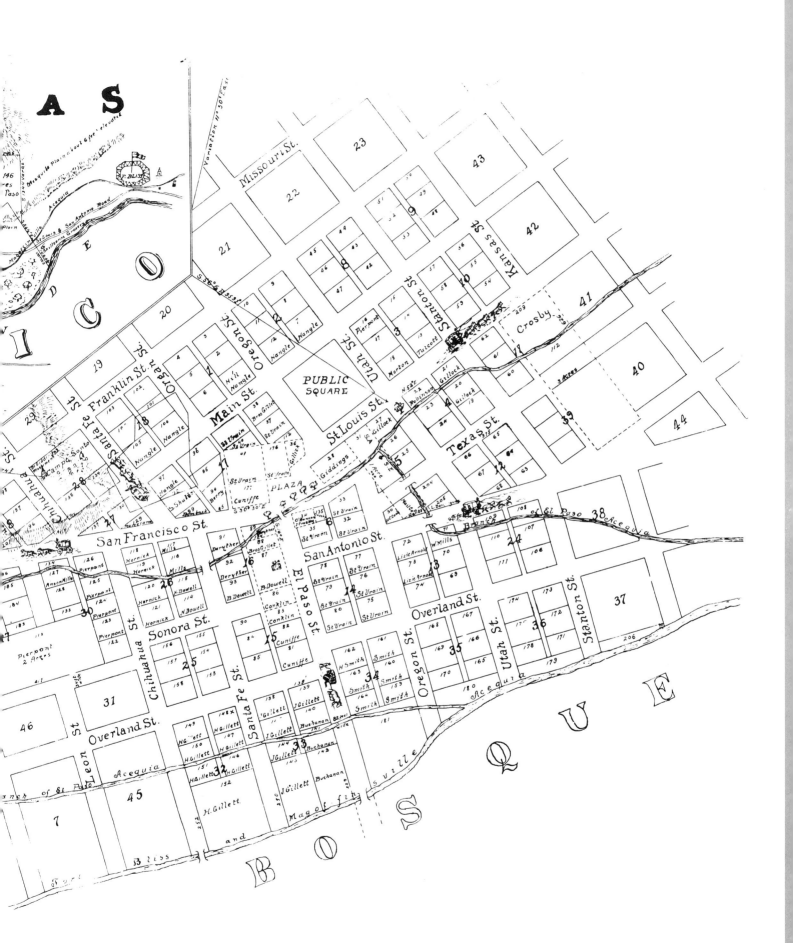

SANTA FE engine No. 246 gets
ready to leave El Paso depot
for New Mexico in 1882. Engineer
Charles Wing, second from left,
stands with his crew.
Today's Santa Fe Freight Office
is at the same location at
Sixth and Santa Fe streets.

Railroads bring
the booming
1880's

EL PASO'S 700 inhabitants—before the iron horses puff their way into town in 1881 —huddle in a collection of mud huts in awesome isolation on the western frontier. The town looks much more Mexican than American. Because of its geography it doesn't have the false-fronted frame buildings and board sidewalks of most struggling western towns. Its architecture is pure Mexican; thick adobe walls and mud roofs. Along El Paso Street (which then extended south from little Pioneer Plaza for about three blocks) heavy, plastered adobe columns and arches create shaded porticos and keep El Pasoans out of the sun. Lumber is a scarce commodity.

And then the railroads arrive. The smoke-belching engines haul a cargo of lumber and people and money and dreams, and the beginnings of a city. The Southern Pacific arrives first

in May, 1881. A month later the population of El Paso doubles. Then comes the Santa Fe, and by the next year the Texas and Pacific begins regular service from Fort Worth to El Paso. Also in 1882 the Mexican Central Railroad is completed and forms a connection with El Paso to Mexico City.

Everything seemed to be happening at once. With the coming of the railroads, new businesses popped up overnight. The dusty streets were crowded to capacity. Even big city luxuries like indoor plumbing, electric lights and gas, and banking facilities made their appearance at the Pass for the first time. A street railway, powered by mule, was launched. Things moved so fast that some of the business establishments were located in tents, and El Paso Street was belly-deep in mud when it rained.

Two weekly newspapers, *The El Paso Times*

23

and the *El Paso Herald,* raced neck-and-neck to be first to hit the street with their maiden editions. In the end, both papers claimed the publishing date of April 2, 1882.

Saloons and gambling halls opened by the dozens, and the town became a Mecca for gunmen, gamblers, fancy women, riff-raff and boomers of all descriptions.

It was a decade of firsts; a magnificent gingerbread courthouse, graceful and ornate, was constructed with bricks made in El Paso. By 1886, the city had gas street lights, two large hotels, telegraph and telephone companies, several lumber yards, an ice plant, a smelter, a water company and many other niceties of civilization that a booming town on the frontier should have—

including churches and schools.

Harper's Magazine expressed the mood of the times in an article about El Paso in 1885. On a trip by rail along the Rio Grande the writer said, "This country seemed very remote and foreign four years ago, but now the tourist dashes through it on the Pacific express, marveling at all the un-American-looking things to be seen from the car window, everything so different from the sights of the accustomed Western regions bordering the old transcontinental railroad line. Where, only a few months before, the complaining 'tenderfoot' was cursing the miserable fare of the country, the tourist breakfasts, dines, and sups leisurely at a succession of cheerful railway hotels . . . Everywhere are signs of an

HOUSES WERE SCARCE north of downtown in 1887. Montana Street is at right, disappearing into the sandhills about where the YMCA is now. Houses in the foreground face Oregon Street. At left center, Rio Grande Street is hardly more than a dirt path. The Ernest Krause home, near center of the picture at 906 North Stanton, was torn down in 1969, and its distinctive gingerbread rooftop installed in La Villita Shopping Center.

awakened, stirring life, which has changed the country as in the twinkling of an eye.

"The mountains skirting either side of the broad valley draw near together as El Paso is approached, and the train is passing beside the river through a wild gorge . . . Passing Fort Bliss, we alight in El Paso, and step into a drift of light sand almost as fine as ashes . . . The fine sand prevailing everywhere is the great drawback to comfort. One has to wade through it almost ankle-deep in some places, and the carriages send up clouds of suffocating dust. The massive adobe buildings, with arched colonnades over the sidewalks, as in many Italian cities, give parts of the town considerable picturesqueness . . . High mountains slope back from either side of the river. They are grand in aspect, . . . stern and unrelenting, bristling with nude crags that pierce the hot sky.

"El Paso is now a great railroad centre, and therefore promises to become an important city. The published plan of the townsite of El Paso shows that its people have great expectations. The projected rectangular streets gridiron the desolate waste of foothills—at present a regular Sahara—occupying space enough for a second Chicago."

Such was El Paso at the end of the eighties. Booming, lively, vital. The population had jumped to 10,000 and new people were arriving everyday. The little adobe town was beginning to look like a city.

LONGHORN STEERS were familiar sights on El Paso streets in the early 1880's.
Top photo shows the Central Hotel at the head of El Paso Street. The picture below was
taken in 1881 from the balcony of the same building looking south.

IN 1885, *Harper's Monthly* published this engraving and described El Paso as looking more Mexican than American.

COVERED WAGONS and longhorn steers still dominated El Paso Street (below) in 1885. Note that new substantial brick buildings have been built and the town seems completely changed since the 1881 photo on the opposite page.

The gunfighters arrive

GUNFIGHT in progress gets full attention of onlookers in front of El Popular Saloon at Seventh and El Paso streets at the turn of the century. The buildings shown here were torn down in the late 1960's to make room for new U.S. Customs facilities.

TWO-GUN MARSHAL Dallas Stoudenmire was a giant figure at six feet, four inches. This picture was taken in 1881 shortly after he was hired to clean up El Paso.

Up until the 1880's El Paso was a frontier town; woolly, but not very wild. It was just too little. It took the coming of the railroads and civilization to make it both woolly *and* wild. Back in 1881, streets like San Antonio and El Paso had the rowdy look of carnival midways, with rows of noisy, brightly lit saloons and dance halls lining the boardwalk on both sides of the streets. And it was partly this appeal that attracted hardcase characters from all over the West. The life style had its fascination for the fast guns and they came to El Paso in large numbers. The town was frequented by some of the biggest names in the business; Billy the Kid, John Wesley Hardin, Wyatt Earp, Dallas Stoudenmire, John Selman, Bat Masterson and Pat Garrett. Even Calamity Jane got married in El Paso to a hack driver named Burke in 1886.

28

PAT GARRETT became famous after killing Billy the Kid in 1881 and collected the grand total of $500 from the State of New Mexico. Garrett later became Collector of Customs in El Paso.

DALLAS STOUDENMIRE'S pistols—.44 Colts—were given by El Paso Marshal James B. Gillett to Sul Ross College in Alpine, Texas.

LOOKING NORTH from the corner of Overland and South El Paso Street (above) shows the beginning of El Paso's building boom. In 1882, plastered adobe buildings gave way to American brick and wood. San Jacinto Plaza (below) begins to take shape in 1884 with desert planting and a pool in the center.

MULE CAR makes its appearance in this 1884 photo of the Bassett Lumber yard at the corner of Mills and Stanton streets. The new State National Bank occupies this corner today.

HOUCK AND DIETER soda pop bottle dating back to the early 1880's was unearthed during excavation for the civic center. UTEP archaeologists also traced the route of the original acequia along San Francisco Street in the civic center area. About 1885, the acequia was filled in and buildings were built on top of it when El Paso's first water wells were drilled.

ST. CLEMENTS Episcopal Church was organized in the 1870's. The picture below shows the church as it looked about 1885 in the 200 block of North Mesa, just north of the present Walgreens Drug Store.

THE EL PASO TIMES was published in this frame building in the early 1880's on Mills Street across from the Plaza.

MESA GARDEN was a popular social gathering place for El Pasoans. It overlooked the whole city from a hill near West Yandell and Rio Grande Street, and is now the site of the Diplomat Apartments, next to the home of Mrs. J. Burges Perrenot.

Satterthwaite's Addition

Soon after the railroads caused El Paso's first boom, a few farsighted El Pasoans began looking cautiously toward the horizon — away from the tight little settlement that had sprung up around the Plaza. One of these citizens was a New Yorker named J. Fisher Satterthwaite. In the early 1800's he was El Paso's Park and Street Commissioner. He plotted San Jacinto Plaza, planted the trees, built the first fountain and installed the first alligators. All this he did at his own expense — as his salary from the city was only $50 a year.

In 1883 and 1884 he developed one of El Paso's first "additions" which later was to become Sunset Heights. At that time, however, it was known as Satterthwaite's Addition. In 1884, Satterthwaite proclaimed: "The owner has graded in a first class manner all of the main streets and has made a rule never to sell lots except on graded streets. Some of these streets are brought to as true a grade as any in the Eastern cities and are ready for the horse car tracks . . . The owner would state to the public that when Map No. 1 of his Addition was published a year since, few houses were on his Addition, and that now over eighty houses are there, and that his claim made then, that as his Addition comprised all the high land in the city, the residences would principally go in that direction, has been verified."

Naturally, lots of El Paso folks laughed at J. Fisher Satterthwaite in 1884. The town would just never go all the way up on top of those hills. Too far from downtown. But then people said about the same thing in the late 1940's when the city's first major post-war subdivision, Loretto Place, filled up. Most people thought El Paso was, as they said, "overbuilt".

SOUTHERN PACIFIC DEPOT, as it looked in the early 1880's, was located on Main Street between Stanton and Kansas streets. On top of the hill in the distance is famous Mesa Garden.

SATTERTHWAITE'S Addition, later changed to Sunset Heights, was brand new when this picture was made about 1885 on what became known as "McGinty Hill".

JUAREZ CUSTOM HOUSE with its charming
Victorian look was built in 1889. This steel engraving shows an El Paso
mule car on 16th of September Street.

STANTON STREET BRIDGE across the Rio Grande was
erected in 1882 and was the first pedestrian and vehicular bridge to span
the river. This picture was taken about 1885 from the Mexican
side looking toward Mt. Franklin.

SOUTHERN PACIFIC DEPOT
about 1885. The sign
on front reads: To San
Francisco 1285 miles,
To New Orleans 1208 miles.

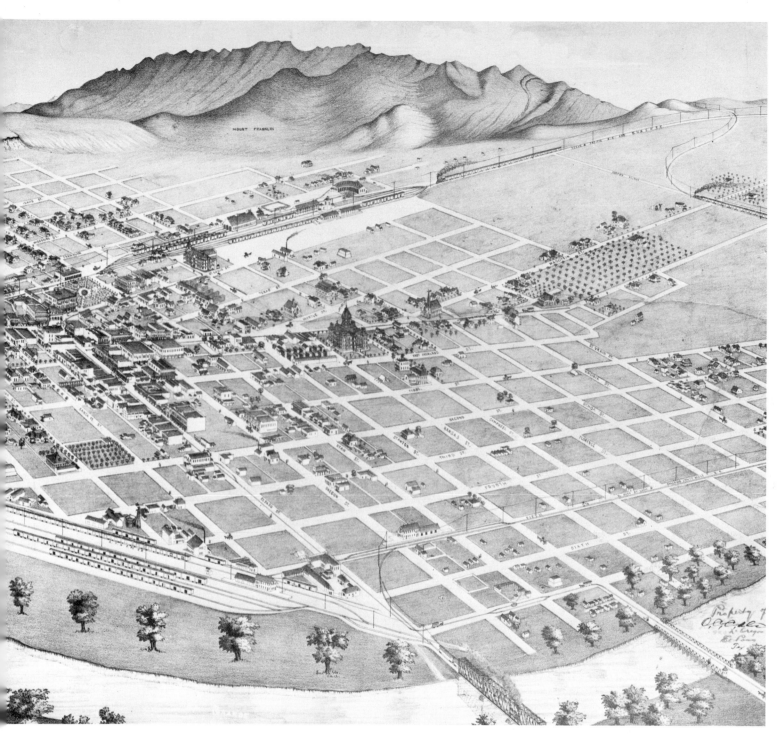

BIRD'S EYE VIEW of El Paso
in 1885 shows several houses
pushing out toward Cotton Avenue,
but beyond that nothing
but desert. Montana Street extends
only seven blocks.

EL PASO STREET in 1884
was beginning to look quite
respectable. The Central Hotel at
left center is the present site of
the White House Department Store.

35

MAGNIFICENT was the word they
used to describe El Paso's
Grand Central Hotel, built in 1883
by Josiah Crosby and Anson Mills.

BUSINESSES at San Antonio
Street and Mesa Avenue
were shaded by tall cottonwoods
in this contemporary woodcut
of the scene published in 1882.

36

MT. FRANKLIN looks lonesome in
this unusual picture; no town, no
streets and only five adobe shacks.

THIS BUILDING was erected
in the mid-1880's and named
Center Block because it was at the
center of town at the corner
of El Paso and San Francisco streets.
It later became the *El Paso Herald*
Building, and the corner is now
occupied by the Oasis Restaurant.

37

RED BRICK and high-steepled
Union Depot opened in 1906.
Note the buggies at left and the
streetcar waiting to pick up
passengers from trains. In the early
1940's the building was remodeled
to give it a Spanish appearance by
removing the steep roof line and
covering the old brick with stucco.

The century turns and El Paso becomes a city

BY the end of the 1880's most of the woolly
western towns present pretty respectable
faces to the world. The shoot-outs at high noon
in the middle of dusty streets surrender to judges
and juries and policemen, and the drama is
preserved in faded library copies of frontier newspapers for future generations to recreate on television. Railroads ship cattle by fast rail instead
of the long drive up the cattle trails from Texas.
Even the lusty towns like Dodge City and Abi-
lene, at the end of the Texas cattle trails, begin
to take on an air of respectability.

But El Paso is different. As always, because
of its isolation, change comes slowly. As other
towns boom and die or tighten their laws, the
riff-raff and the gamblers and the pistoleros drift
away. And a lot of them drift to El Paso where

the law stretches pretty thin. In the 1890's, El
Paso provides plenty of action, and if one of the
town's new citizens happens to be on the dodge,
the comparative safety of Mexico lies just a
splash across the Rio Grande.

These were the hey-days of fast-draw artists
like John Wesley Hardin, who moved to El Paso
in 1895 with the reputation of having killed forty
men. Hardin's trail played out in the Acme Saloon one night when he got himself shot through
the back of the head by John Selman, the constable of Justice Precinct 1. Selman was reputed
to be "king of the quick deadshots of the Southwest" and was also known around the territory
as a rustler, a robber and a killer. For a short
time he was famous as the "man who killed John
Wesley Hardin", but the old constable didn't

keep his crown very long. In 1896, Selman himself was shot to death by another peace officer, George Scarborough, the Deputy U.S. Marshal headquartered in El Paso.

In the meantime, however, most El Pasoans went about their businesses as peacefully as they could; they didn't carry guns, and never fired a shot at anybody. By 1900, even El Paso was beginning to shed some of its frontier look. It now could boast of a population of 15,000 people. Adobe was giving way rapidly to brick, and handsome buildings were springing up all over town.

A respectable group of citizens called the Citizens League led a reform movement to close the saloons on Sunday and to move gambling from the saloons into basements or upstairs rooms. Sheriff J. H. Boone put some long sharp teeth in the ordinance that called for people to leave their pistols at home unless they had a special permit to carry arms. By 1905, the Citizens League won its battle against the lawless element. Open gambling disappeared from El Paso and another chapter of frontier life ended.

DURING these years a new phase of life in El Paso was beginning—the series of real estate developments that were to settle what is now northeast El Paso. As early as 1890, the Army began to look for a new site for Fort Bliss. The post then was located west of town at Hart's Mill, overlooking the gorge of the Rio Grande. The military had a major problem at this location, however; the main line of the Santa Fe Railroad ran the entire length of the parade ground, a good reason for the post to be moved to its present site on the rim of a great sand-and-cactus-covered mesa overlooking the city from the east.

With the move accomplished in 1893, the city began to take giant strides eastward. Government Hill and Grandview additions were filed officially in 1906. The following year Frank R. Tobin built a railroad line to a new townsite called, naturally, "Tobin". The area was the present intersection of Railroad Drive and Hondo Pass. Tobin divided the town into building sites and established a post office, a light plant, and a fire department. He was a man of vision, but, unfortunately, his town was too far away. As it turned out, he was just about a half century ahead of his time. He also platted and sold land successfully around Washington Park. Lots in Sunset Heights were selling rapidly, and the area east of the downtown section—on San Antonio, Magoffin and Myrtle streets—boasted some of El Paso's finest homes. The St. Regis Hotel opened for business across from San Jacinto Plaza in 1905 and is still operating.

The Happy Hour Theater advertised "polite vaudeville" and the top price for admission was thirty cents.

Until one warm September day in 1906, no one traveled a paved street or walked on a sidewalk in all of El Paso. Complaints about the dusty and sometimes muddy streets became so numerous that the city fathers decided to do something about it. Paving came first to a whole block on Mesa Avenue on the east side of San Jacinto Plaza. Within a few months the central part of the city had both paved streets and sidewalks, paid for by property assessments. In 1908, the City Engineer reported 374 cars in the city, and he asked for better streets to keep the automobiles from being broken up in the deep ruts and potholes.

AT the turn of the century, while El Paso was spreading out to the east, its citizens were enjoying imported culture and the finer things of civilization from back East. Myar's Opera House, located on South El Paso Street just one door south of the St. Charles Hotel (which is the oldest hotel still in business today), was an opulent building opened in 1887. Myar's treated early El Pasoans to theater and music featuring top stars like Sarah Bernhardt. Also elegant and plush for its day was the Chopin Music Hall, on Myrtle Avenue between Campbell and Kansas streets, the present site of the United States Federal Courthouse. Famous Mesa Garden, a favorite spot for a cool drink, perched on top of a hill overlooking the entire city. Mesa Garden was on West Yandell at the present location of the Diplomat Apartments and next to the home of Mrs. J. Burges Perrenot. Probably El Paso's most widely acclaimed organization at the turn of the century was a group of musicians and beer drinkers who called themselves the McGinty Club. On picnics to Washington Park they hauled countless kegs of El Paso beer and they provided many hours of entertainment for fellow El Pasoans. The club died a natural death about 1905 when the national service clubs began to make inroads, but the fame of the McGinty Club lingers on.

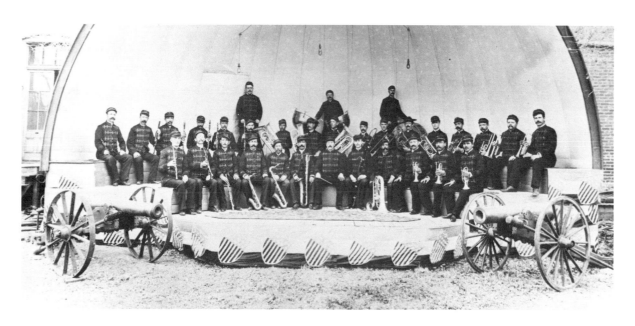

FAMOUS MC GINTY BAND provided entertainment for El Pasoans at the turn of the century. One of these Civil War cannons (in foreground) was stolen by rebels during the Mexican Revolution of 1910 and used against Federal troops. It was finally retrieved by Americans and placed in San Jacinto Plaza for a time, then later donated to a scrap drive during World War II. The other cannon is now proudly on display in the quadrangle at Eastwood High School. Below, five El Paso bakery wagons line up for a picture on North Oregon Street about 1905.

Frank Tobin's townsite was just too far away

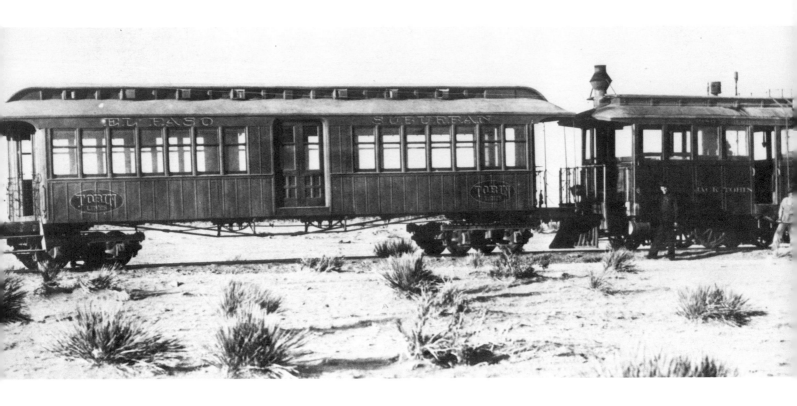

RARE PICTURE of the El Paso
Suburban, a railway built by Frank
Tobin to his ill-fated townsite
in 1907.

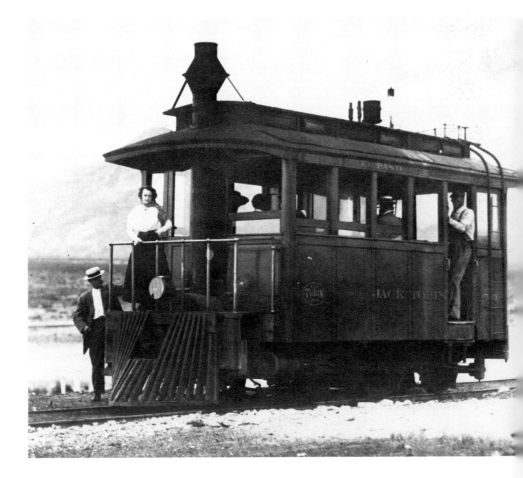

TOBIN'S LOCOMOTIVE stops
on the way back to El Paso
from the townsite of Tobin. The
development was too far away
at the turn of the century, but it
came into its own during the building
boom of the 1950's.

TREE-SHADED streets and the
leisurely pace of mule cars and
bicycles bring back nostalgia for the
El Paso of the 1890's. Above,
the First Baptist Church was an
impressive structure at the
intersection of Magoffin Avenue
(at left) and San Antonio Street.

UNION LABOR parade brought
out lots of spectators to look at
the horseless carriages in 1905. Cars
in the foreground are in front
of what is now the Capri Theater.

HORSEPOWER helps Sunset Heights take shape in 1898. This picture was taken from the corner of Upson and Fewel looking west. At far left is the then H. M. Mundy home at 1401 West Yandell Boulevard and Mundy Avenue. The utility poles at right are along West Yandell. The Mundy home, with the cone towers, still stands.

ASSAY OFFICE at the corner of San Francisco and Chihuahua streets was the birthplace of the McGinty Club, an early musical and social group. Dan Reckhart was president of the club.

TEMPLE MT. SINAI, at Oregon Street and Yandell Boulevard, was built in 1889. The ornate dome was later removed and the building was home for a series of businesses, including the Teen Canteen during World War II. The old temple was torn down in 1963 and is now the site of Rogers and Belding Real Estate and Insurance Company.

THE WHITE HOUSE published this attractive fashion catalog in 1904. Below, Ernst Kohlberg poses with a wooden Indian in front of his International Cigar Factory. Kohlberg's granddaughter is Mrs. Leonard Goodman, Jr.

ONE OF EL PASO's first artists and most popular characters was a one-legged sign painter named Peg Grandover. His shop was located at 412 South El Paso Street.

THE EXCURSION TRAIN puffs its way onto the sixty-foot high trestle and the famous S curve before arriving at Cloudcroft.

Excursions to the clouds

Back in 1900, there were no evaporative coolers to relieve El Paso's summer heat. On summer evenings, aside from sitting on the front porch and fanning a lot, there just wasn't much a person could do about it. Until they built the railroad to Cloudcroft, that is. The cool pines of New Mexico's Sacramento Mountains lay only a hundred miles away, but until the Alamogordo and Sacramento Mountain Railway was completed in 1899, the mountain air might as well have been on the moon.

The Cloudcroft Lodge was built in 1901, and the little resort community got off to a lively start with lots selling for $50 to $250 each. In those days it was possible to build a four-room cabin for about $200.

El Pasoans flocked to build cabins in Cloudcroft, and many of their families still enjoy summer living in some of the turn-of-the-century cottages under the tall pines. Others took advantage of the little excursion train and just went to Cloudcroft on weekends. Open-air excursion cars brought them up from the desert heat, five thousand feet below. And there was always a large crowd waiting at the Cloudcroft Depot for the little train to come in, bringing

OPEN EXCURSION cars were a treat for El Pasoans going to Cloudcroft to escape the summer heat. Canvas side curtains were rolled down when mountain thunderstorms hit unexpectedly.

CLOUDCROFT DEPOT was always crowded to greet the new arrivals when the little yellow excursion cars arrived from El Paso.

a new load of visitors. An advertisement in *The El Paso Times* of August 31, 1907, quoted a price of three dollars for the round trip Labor Day excursion to Cloudcroft. For no extra charge, an army band from Fort Bliss accompanied the excursion and remained in Cloudcroft for a Labor Day band concert, a turn-of-the-century fringe benefit.

For more than three decades excursion trips on the little yellow cars were a way of life for El Pasoans in the summertime. In the 1920's the train would stop at Piedras Street on its way back to the depot and let people off who lived in that part of town. But by 1930, the popular excursions were terminated, and regular trains ran only three times a week. In time, uncomplaining passengers were happy to ride even the caboose, and after 1938 the railroad hauled only freight; no passengers or mail. In 1947, the last scheduled train came down from Cloudcroft and crews started pulling up the tracks. It wasn't until the early 1950's that the narrow dirt road up into the mountains was paved from Alamogordo to Cloudcroft, following for many miles the original roadbed of the little railroad into the mountains. The weathered timbers from the old trestles can still be seen along the highway east of Cloudcroft.

The 1890's: last grand stand of the gunfighters

GAMBLING was a twenty-four-hour-a-day attraction in El Paso saloons during the 1890's. The last of the old gunmen came to El Paso when most of the West was no longer wild. But in El Paso it was still the hey-day of the fast-draw artists.

JOHN WESLEY HARDIN moved to El Paso in 1895 with the reputation of having killed forty men. This picture was taken shortly before he got himself shot through the back of the head in the Acme Saloon, which was located near the corner of San Antonio Street and Mesa Avenue where Lerner's is today.

JOHN SELMAN, El Paso constable, became famous as the man who killed John Wesley Hardin.

TEXAS RANGERS helped keep the peace in El Paso when this picture was taken in 1896.
Second from left (front row) is El Paso's famous Ranger Captain John R. Hughes.

HAND GUN ARTIST Jeff Milton (left) was El Paso's City Marshal in 1894 and George
Scarborough (right) was Deputy United States Marshal during a period of reform activity.
Both men had massive reputations before coming to El Paso.

MOST IMPOSING STRUCTURE in El Paso in 1896 was this Victorian-style County Courthouse, located on the same spot as today's City-County Building.

It was a splendid time

JUAREZ CUSTOM HOUSE faced unpaved 16th of September Street in 1907.

At the turn of the century, El Pasoans exuded optimism and self-confidence. They had faith in the city and felt that progress was inevitable. Opportunities abounded on all sides as El Paso moved into the 20th Century, and the population zoomed to 39,000 by 1910. The city at the Pass was a far cry from the adobe village of 700 inhabitants hugging the river's edge only thirty years before.

HAPPY HOUR THEATER on South El Paso Street packed them in during the early 1900's. It was razed about 1911 to make way for construction of Hotel Paso del Norte.

SAN JACINTO PLAZA provided a shady oasis for El Pasoans at the turn of the century.

They painted signs and paved the streets

OUTDOOR ADVERTISING was painted on every available spot in in the early 1900's. This is the corner of Mesa and Mills, now the site of the Roberts-Banner Building. Note the small sign at top center reading "McClintock Co.". Advertisements painted by this early sign company are still visible today on some buildings in El Paso.

OPEN AIR STREETCAR crosses the Santa Fe Street Bridge from Juarez to El Paso about 1902.

FIRST PAVING of an El Paso street took place on Mesa Avenue on the east side of San Jacinto Plaza. In this picture, Adele Fewel starts it all as she breaks a bottle of champagne over the side of a paving machine in front of the old Orndorff Hotel. The year was 1906.

JUAREZ MISSION, built in 1659, looked like this in 1896. In the foreground is 16th of September Street.

ST. CHARLES HOTEL on the southwest corner of South El Paso and Overland streets is El Paso's oldest hotel still in business.

EL PASO'S FIRST STEEL framework goes up in 1906. This was the El Paso and Southwestern Railroad Building on Stanton and Franklin streets. It later became the Southern Pacific Building and is now the American Bank of Commerce. Below, Mandy the Mule gets a free ride as El Paso celebrates the coming of electric streetcars in 1902. Previously, cars were pulled by mules.

MULE CARS like these provided transportation for El Pasoans from 1882 until 1902 when electric streetcars took over.

SAN ANTONIO STREET looking east sported buggies, electric car tracks and a banner advertising the Volunteer Fire Department's Spring Festival in the early 1900's. At right is the Wigwam Saloon, which later became a theater and is now the State Theater.

EL PASO HIGH SCHOOL in 1902 was located at Arizona
and Campbell streets. It later became Morehead School and is now the site
of Hotel Dieu School of Nursing.

COOL, SHADY VERANDAS were trademarks of the Orndorff Hotel across from the Plaza.
This later became the site of the Cortez Hotel.

WINTER SCENE of San Jacinto Plaza shows the bandstand and alligator pool about 1900. In the center, across Main Street a horse can be seen tied behind a residence. Note that both Oregon Street (at left) and Mesa Street (at right) seem to run out of town and stop before reaching the mesa in the background.

PIONEER El Pasoan Ernst Kohlberg and his family lived in this brick home on Oregon Street and Yandell Boulevard at the turn of the century. Note the wood sidewalks and high wheel bicycle.

THIS UNUSUAL PHOTOGRAPH shows El Paso's ornate old courthouse surrounded by newly-completed courthouse in 1916. The J. E. Morgan contracting firm built the new building around the old, then razed the old one to make way for Liberty Hall.

four

The
turbulent
teens

HECTIC change marks the second decade of the century. El Paso's population mushrooms, and El Pasoans struggle to catch up with modern times. Gone now are the dusty streets and board sidewalks that had made El Paso feel and look like a frontier town. Gone are most of the hitching posts and saddle horses. The old-time guns and tinhorns fade into oblivion and become bad guys and good guys in dime novels. But you can still buy a glass of beer for a nickel, with a free lunch on the side.

El Paso was trying to catch up with the twentieth century. It was the age of Henry Ford's Tin Lizzie. His Model T began to rattle around the streets, and El Pasoans bought them by the hundreds for $360 apiece. The real estate boom continued; Manhattan Heights subdivision was filed in 1912, Morningside Heights in 1913, Kern Place in 1914, Summit Place in 1915 and

Highland Park in 1919.

El Paso also bred its share of land speculators, and hundreds of "view" lots were sold by promoters to unsuspecting buyers from out of town. Hollywood Heights, a subdivision filed in 1917, was a classic example. It is still shown on city maps today and is better known to the natives as Sugarloaf Peak at the entrance to McKelligon Canyon. Another mountainside development was known as Rosemont Addition. It, too, was filed in 1917 and was laid out in the arroyos and sheer red cliffs leading from the end of McKinley Street to the top of Mt. Franklin.

More and more streets got paved, and the paving mania grew until in 1916 El Paso led all other American cities by laying eight miles of bitulithic pavement in a single year at a cost of $390,000. The city provided street name signs for the first time in 1915.

IT was a decade of constructing major buildings which are still part of the El Paso skyline. The Mills Building was completed in 1911, and was followed a year later by the grand opening of Hotel Paso del Norte on the site once occupied by a vaudeville house, The Happy Hour Theater. The White House Department Store moved into its present location the same year.

In 1916, El Paso High School and the Popular Dry Goods Company were both under construction. Also that year, the Texas State School of Mines and Metallurgy moved to what was thought of as a northwest site. The school had opened two years earlier near Fort Bliss and a disastrous fire caused the move from the east to the west side of the mountain. By the end of 1917, the first two structures, the former Chemistry and Main buildings, were completed and enrollment for the 1917-1918 year reached the grand total of sixty-one. The new County Courthouse replaced the old ornate 19th Century courthouse, and in 1918, a new auditorium was completed, between the two wings of the courthouse. The first gathering was for the purpose of selling Liberty Bonds for the war effort. After this patriotic meeting the auditorium was named Liberty Hall.

The decade of the teens wrote one of the biggest single chapters in the history of El Paso and Juarez. That was the building of Elephant Butte Dam. For years the towns that straddled the Rio Grande at the Pass fought flood waters during spring and summer runoffs from up river. As early as 1886 *The El Paso Times* reported that "at Anthony the river was about three miles wide, of which the regular river bed was about twelve feet deep and remainder between two and four feet." Then, in 1888, the whole area was hit by a throat-parching drought. Thousands of fruit trees died, and the vineyards that had furnished grapes for the then-famous El Paso wine died in the blistering heat. The flood of 1897 all but washed both towns away. The city fathers asked Anson Mills to come up with a plan to relieve the water situation. He immediately suggested that a dam be built on the Rio Grande— to be located about three miles above the city, about where the Southwestern Portland Cement Company is now located. It would have flooded the valley for about fifteen miles north.

Nobody, including the states of New Mexico and Colorado could agree on the site of the proposed dam, and it wasn't until 1907 that the dam, to be located near Hot Springs, New Mexico, was authorized by Congress. Construction started in 1912, and the job was finished in 1916. It was then that cotton was introduced to the irrigated valleys, and agriculture in the El Paso valley became a stable contributor to the city's economy.

DURING these years, the Mexican Revolution and its resulting border problems brought thousands of new troops to Fort Bliss. Even before America's entry into World War I, El Paso began to literally burst at the seams. The military population of Fort Bliss, with some of its tented camps reaching nearly all the way south to the Rio Grande expanded to accommodate more than 45,000 men.

AUTOMOBILES replaced horses on El Paso streets in the 1910-1920 decade. During the transition this fringe-topped bus hauled tourists to Juarez.

THE WHITE HOUSE Department Store was an elegant addition to the skyline shortly after the grand opening of its new quarters in 1912.

61

KERN PLACE takes shape in 1916. This was El Paso's first subdivision to have curvilinear streets. The house in the center of this picture is located at 1019 Robinson. The street in the foreground is Madeline, at the intersection of Piedmont. Kern Place arch spanned North Kansas Street at Robinson Street in 1916. This fantastic array of lights and piping was designed by developer Pete Kern.

SUBSTANTIAL HOMES
appeared during the building boom
in east El Paso between 1910
and 1920. The two-story
houses above are at the corner of
Elm and San Diego streets.

FEDERAL BUILDING at the
corner of Oregon and Mills streets
was built in 1890. It served
El Paso well for many years as a
courthouse, as well as the location of
the Custom House, Post Office and Weather
Bureau. It was razed in 1936 to
make way for the present Kress store.

ELEGANT WINDOW DISPLAY marked the grand opening of The White House Department Store in 1912.

THE POPULAR Dry Goods Company as it looked during World War I days. At left is the corner of Mesa Avenue and San Antonio Street, the same location occupied by the Popular today.

An intrepid birdman flies in Washington Park

CHARLES HAMILTON gets a push from Washington Park ground crew. This old Curtiss biplane lifted him and the airplane off the ground and into local immortality as the first man ever to fly in El Paso. The year was 1910. Below, U.S. Cavalry horses are startled by kite-looking craft as it becomes airborne in El Paso's lower valley.

CROCKETT SCHOOL was way out in the sandhills when this picture was taken.
The school opened its doors in 1920 and was called Manhattan Heights School until 1922.
Memorial Park now occupies the land in the foreground. Below, El Paso High School
was under construction in 1916.

NEW HIGH SCHOOL
TROST & TROST ARCHITECTS.
J.E. MORGAN. CONTRACTOR.

THESE BIG electric cars were familiar sights in the lower valley until 1925.

The interurban to Ysleta

Transportation from downtown to the Lower Valley presented a major problem to El Pasoans and they began to push for an interurban trolley, the period's most popular mode of urban travel. A firm, called the Rio Grande Valley Traction Co., was organized to construct and operate the line, and on August 27, 1913, opening day festivities of the interurban line were reported by

The El Paso Times. More than 100 of El Paso's leading businessmen made the first trip to Ysleta in 40 minutes. The high-speed cars ran sixty miles an hour, had upholstered cushions and a separate smoking compartment with swinging doors. The interurban is still remembered fondly by many El Pasoans, and it served them well until 1925 when the electric cars gave way to buses.

From carriage to horseless carriage in a decade

HORSE-DRAWN vehicles were abundant in 1911. This picture above shows the corner of Mesa and Mills, and except for the horses and buggies, it looks much the same today. Below is the same corner several years later. Automobiles have replaced most of the buggies.

THE TRANSITION from horses to autos is evident in this 1912 picture of Longwell's Transfer near the corner of San Francisco and Santa Fe streets. At the time, Longwell's was just growing out of a livery stable, as its signs show.

ONE OF EL PASO'S first electric cars was owned by Dr. and Mrs. A. R. Klein, parents of Mrs. Mike Brumbelow. Note that Montana Street was still unpaved when this picture was taken about 1910. In the background is the Turney home, which later became El Paso Museum of Art.

EL PASO'S newly-built skyline forms a substantial backdrop for San Jacinto Plaza in 1911. Note Mills Building under construction at right.

ORIGINAL El Paso-Pecos Valley Bus Line followed dirt trails all the way to Artesia, New Mexico.

STOP AND GO signals were hand-operated as the horse and buggy age became the automobile age. The policeman stands on Mills Street.

UNIFORMED DRIVERS stand in front of the Popular Dry Goods Company's new delivery truck fleet about 1915.

ELEPHANT BUTTE DAM construction began in 1912. At left is the Rio Grande running near the base of Elephant Butte. The buildings shown here were covered by the lake when the dam was completed in 1916.

The movie houses: a touch of elegance

A FAVORITE downtown movie house was the Unique, one door north of the Hotel Paso del Norte at 111 South El Paso Street. This building is still very recognizable today.

THE BIJOU was at 212 South El Paso Street. The United Army Supply has occupied this building for many years.

THE WIGWAM Theater grew out of a turn-of-the-century saloon and gambling hall. Many El Pasoans can remember watching serials on Saturday afternoons at the Wigwam. It is now the State Theater.

LAVISH MOORISH architecture dominated the Alhambra Theater, a downtown movie house on South El Paso Street. Its name was later changed to the Palace, and it is doing business today at the same location. The fancy exterior filigree work can still be seen.

OPTIMISM in El Paso's future is depicted in this 1911 dream-like painting
of the city's future appearance. Note the subway entrance at the bottom left and
tree-shaded San Jacinto Plaza in middleground. This illustration
appeared in the 1911 Chamber of Commerce annual report.

It had been quite a decade

The teen years saw the population of El Paso
spurt to more than 77,000 by 1920—almost double
what it had been at the beginning of the decade.
A massive influx of refugees from Mexico and its
Revolution was responsible for much of the population explosion. El Pasoans watched their streets
change from dirt to pavement; they saw the horse
give way to the automobile and they even got a
preview of the airplane. The old days were gone
at last, and by 1920 the frontier was just a memory.

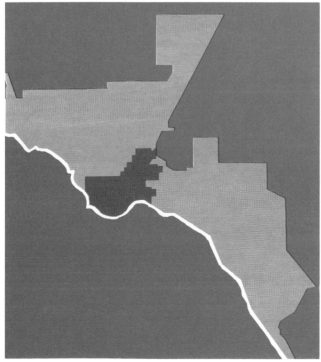

SHELDON HOTEL was built in
1887 and remained a famous
landmark until it burned in 1929. It
was replaced by the Hilton Hotel
in 1930.

CITY LIMITS in 1919 included eleven
square miles. The city remained almost the
same size until after World War II.
Map shows 1971 city limits in light gray.

Revolution next door

THE MADERO REVOLUTION, starting in 1910, provided El Pasoans with a first-hand look at war.

THE decade of 1910 to 1920, one of hectic change for El Paso, holds even more exciting and traumatic times for her sister city — Juarez. Ten years of almost constant war and upheaval plague Mexican citizens, but the years pave a rough road leading to equality — an equality Mexicans are still trying to achieve. It is the time of the Mexican Revolution.

Porfirio Diaz rules Mexico in 1910. An old army general who has held the presidency since 1876, Diaz does much to modernize Mexico, to industrialize it, and to give this proud country some political stability. Under his regime a few people acquire great wealth, but the rest of Mexico sinks ever lower into poverty. The eighty-year-old dictator governs with an iron hand, ruthlessly crushing any opposition, controlling the press, and creating a new police force called the rurales to keep the peons in line.

But a frail little Mexican intellectual named Francisco Madero came forward to change all that. Preaching agrarian and political reform, he started an uprising that was to have an impact on the people of Juarez and El Paso for many years, and the state of Chihuahua was to become the storm center of a revolution. The formation of the Madero junta actually took place in El Paso—on the fifth floor of the Caples Building. Arms and ammunition went through El Paso—destined for the growing rebel army in Chihuahua.

BY 1911, it was obvious that El Paso was going to play a big part in the revolution. Since Juarez was the largest Mexican city on the border, its capture was essential to the rebels. Word came that Pascual Orozco, the insurgent chief from the district of Guerrero was gathering for an all-out attack on Juarez. Orozco, with some 1500 men, moved north of Juarez and camped on the Mexican side of the river opposite the El Paso Smelter. Orozco himself visited El Paso while awaiting the battle of Juarez. Meanwhile, Madero's army came up from the south and bivouacked nearby in the same greasewood and rocky arroyos across from the smelter. At this point, a man whose name was to become one of the most famous in Mexican history, Francisco "Pancho" Villa, arrived in Madero's camp with some seven hundred picked men. El Paso had a ringside seat for war, and literally thousands of its citizens crossed the Rio Grande on a swinging foot bridge to visit Madero's headquarters and take pictures of the insurrectos, menacing in their huge hats and bandoliers of ammunition across their chests.

For days in advance, El Paso and Juarez knew the attack was coming, and the roofs and streets of Juarez were thoroughly sandbagged for protection. El Pasoans by the thousands stood on rooftops and hills to watch the fighting. Finally, on May 9, 1911, the rebels jumped off, followed the irrigation ditch leading into Juarez and attacked the city from the north. The battle raged for two days, and El Paso's Mayor Kelly established a line in south El Paso, declaring it off-limits to all Americans. But in spite of precautions, five El Pasoans were killed and fifteen were wounded by stray bullets from across the river before the garrison of Juarez surrendered to the power of Villa and Orozco.

When the news of the capture of Juarez reached Mexico City, mobs rioted in front of the National Palace and demanded Diaz' resignation. A conference was held across from the El Paso Smelter, and Diaz, the fallen dictator, agreed to resign. Shortly afterward he boarded a French crusier at Vera Cruz on his way to exile.

Madero was elected president of Mexico, but peace was not to last for long. No sooner had the forces of the Diaz regime been defeated than a struggle began between the ambitious revolutionary leaders. The next few years provided one counter revolution after another. In 1912, a tough old campaigner named Victoriano Huerta had Madero shot down in cold blood and made himself president. Once again Mexico was wracked by the nightmare of revolution, and the population dropped by almost a million during the decade. For sheer brutality and bloodletting, the Mexican Revolution probably has had no equal, including the Russian Revolution.

BACK across the border, El Paso became an armed camp. Fort Bliss moved troops into the city, National Guard units from many states moved to the border, and Fort Bliss became a major Army post. General John J. Pershing took command and by 1916 a large part of the entire regular army of the United States was on the border. That same year, in one of the few attacks on American territory in history, Pancho Villa's troops rode over the barbed wire fence which served as the border between the United States and Mexico and attacked and burned the tiny New Mexico town of Columbus. Ten days later, five thousand American troops led by General Pershing moved into Mexico with orders to capture Villa. The Punitive Expedition, as it was known, continued to search in vain for the elusive Pancho, giving chase to mounted bands of Villistas that seemed to vanish like mirages into the Sierra Madres they knew so well.

The Punitive Expedition was never able to get Villa in its grasp; it only succeeded in enraging the Mexican government. Negotiations for a peaceful settlement were arranged in El Paso between American General Hugh Scott and the Mexican minister of war, General Alvaro Obregon. In the meetings which were held at Hotel Paso del Norte it was agreed that the United States would withdraw from Mexico. Pershing's expedition was ordered home and his troops came back across the border in 1917. He had been gone eleven months, but the experience he gained in this campaign brought him to the forefront of American military men. After the United States entered World War I that year he was named commander of the American Expeditionary Forces and led American troops—many of them trained along the border—to victory in France. The Mexican Revolution left a far-reaching impact on El Paso by the addition of many thousands of Mexican refugees to its population.

THIS RARE PHOTOGRAPH shows Mexican bandit chief Maximo Castillo leaping from a baggage car during an actual train robbery in Chihuahua. The photographer could easily have been executed on the spot for taking a picture like this.

REBELS move toward Juarez
during the early days of the
Madero revolt.

WIDE-BRIMMED sombreros and
bandoliers of ammunition were
trademarks of the rebels in 1911

80

THESE REBEL TROOPS near Juarez in 1911 look almost as though they were supplied by Central Casting for a Hollywood movie.

PANCHO VILLA (center) purchases a motorcycle in El Paso for his army. Arms, ammunition and supplies for Villa poured through El Paso during the years 1910 to 1920.

MADERO'S HEADQUARTERS across from the El Paso smelter in 1911. At right center is the foot bridge that Americans used to cross the Rio Grande and visit rebel troops.

WAR BY TELEPHONE was carried on for a time between Madero Headquarters across from the smelter and Federal headquarters in Juarez.

PROVISIONAL GOVERNMENT of Mexico in 1911 posed for this official photograph a few feet from U.S. territory. Mopping his brow in center is (1) Francisco Madero, (2) Dr. Francisco Vazquez Gomez, (3) Francisco Madero, Sr., (4) Abraham Gonzalez, (5) Venustiano Carranza, (6) J. la Luz Gonzalez, (7) J. Mayortoreno, (8) Albert Fuentes, (9) Pascual Orozco, (10) Alphonso Madero, (11) Sanchez Ascona, (12) de la Luz Blanco, (13) Federico Gonzalez Garcia, (14) Guiseppe Garibaldi, (15) Gustavo Madero, (16) Pancho Villa.

MT. FRANKLIN looms up behind Madero's headquarters in May, 1911. At left center is the international boundary marker which can still be seen today at this location just south of the brick plant.

REBEL GIRLS accompanied Pancho Villa's troops wherever they went and sometimes actually took part in the battles. They became fabled in song as Las Adelitas.

MOUNTED CAVALRY near Juarez helped rebels oust the government of dictator Porfirio Diaz.

REBEL HORSEMAN gives battle instructions to foot soldiers.

FIELD PIECES like this were few and far between during the Madero revolution. Much combat was hand to hand and unmatched in viciousness.

TRIUMPHANT REVOLUTIONARY TROOPS enter Juarez from the lower valley in 1911. Note the first three horsemen blowing bugles heralding their arrival. The automobile alongside was a new innovation in warfare.

KETELSEN AND DEGETAU, a German-owned general mercantile store was burned to the ground during the Battle of Juarez.

SOON AFTER the Battle of Juarez in 1911, damage was inspected by curious El Pasoans. Thousands of bullet holes perforated the adobe walls (above). Below is the Juarez Post Office which was battered in the bombardment which lasted for several days before the fall of Juarez to rebel troops.

Fort Bliss troops move into position

FORT BLISS CAVALRY TROOPS move up Rio Grande Street in 1916 as protection for the U.S. side of the border. At top center is the home of Senator A. B. Fall on Arizona Street which was rented by the Luis Terrazas family of Chihuahua.

NEGRO INFANTRY troops from Columbus, N.M., set up camp at the foot of the Santa Fe Street Bridge when Villa attacked Juarez in 1919.

AMERICAN TROOPS patrolled the border and El Paso Mayor C. E. Kelly and
Pancho Villa held a meeting on the Stanton Street Bridge to establish amicable relations between
the neighbor cities. Below, Troop H, 8th Cavalry lines up on West San Francisco Street.

REBELS EXECUTE a suspected spy in 1914. Note Mt. Franklin in the background.

Revolution: the ideals get twisted

One after another, the revolutionary leaders turned on each other — Pancho Villa against Venustiano Carranza, Alvaro Obregon against Villa, Obregon against Carranza, Villa and Obregon against Huerta—until not even the Mexicans could understand the baffling situation. To the cry of "Viva Villa!" the revolutionaries threw off the yoke of oppression and went on binges of fighting, drinking, raping, and go-

ing to their deaths without really knowing what they were dying for. Mariano Azuela, who wrote the novel *Los de Abajo* in El Paso in 1915, probably summed up the twisted frustrations of the revolution better than anyone with this passage: "Down in Chihuahua I killed a man because I always saw him sitting at the table whenever I went to eat. I hated the looks of him so I just killed him! What the hell could I do!"

SIGHTS like this were familiar along the route of the Mexican Central Railway through northern Chihuahua.

REBEL OFFICER, at left with sword, gives orders to fire during fighting in Juarez.

REBELS bundle up with blankets and overcoats during fighting in northern Chihuahua winter. Some rebels had never before been away from tropical Mexico.

AMERICAN GENERAL Hugh Scott was sent to the border by President Woodrow Wilson to meet with Pancho Villa in an effort to effect peace between Villa and Carranza. Generals Scott and Villa (in center) are shown here on the international bridge. At the far right is Rodolfo Fierro, Villa's right-hand man who was also known as "the butcher" for his ruthlessness.

MEXICAN FEDERAL Army officers had uniforms and style similar to Europeans.

BUFFALO BILL Cody visits Fort Bliss in 1915.

Chihuahua's railroads: prime targets for the rebels

FROM 1910 to 1920 hundreds of bridges were burned on the Mexico Northwestern Railway. Entire trains were destroyed by rebels and bandits. Locomotives were run into open bridges, diverted down the sides of steep canyons in the Sierra Madres. Freight cars and passenger coaches were burned, dynamited and turned loose down steep grades. Station buildings and water tanks were destroyed and telephone lines were cut periodically. In the picture below mounted rebels survey damage after dynamiting a train.

The refugees head for El Paso and safety

PRIVATE STAGECOACH of General Luis Terrazas, Governor of Chihuahua, as he prepares to flee from rebel troops when Villa took Chihuahua City.

GENERAL TERRAZAS reports to American Army officers after crossing the Rio Grande to safety.

WELL-DRESSED American refugees struggle across the desert heading for the safety of El Paso.

MULE TEAM pulls this touring car across the Rio Grande one jump ahead of Villa.

MEXICAN REFUGEES arrive at Fort Bliss where the American Army set up a refugee camp.

95

MORMON REFUGEES from their colonies in northern Chihuahua set up housekeeping in an El Paso lumber yard.

U.S. CAVALRY troops were stationed at Columbus, New Mexico, in 1916.
That year, nearly the entire regular army of the United States was either on the border or with Pershing's expedition into Mexico.

Bows and arrows were still around in 1910

TARAHUMARA INDIANS from Chihuahua joined the rebel army in 1910. These barefooted soldiers wore loin cloths and straw hats and most of them had only bows and arrows for weapons against federal troops.

THE WILD WEST and Indian wars seemed a long way off to most parts of the United States in the decade of 1910 to 1920. But the Mexican Border still had the look of the western frontier as this old photo shows.

DURING PROHIBITION Juarez put out the welcome mat with bars like the
Big Kid's near 16th of September and Lerdo streets. The Big Kid's advertised "the longest bar,
the best beer and the most booze."

98

six

The twenties roared

IN 1920, El Paso seems peaceful at last. World
War I is over, and many of the ex-dough-
boys who saw duty on the border come back to
El Paso to make their homes in the Southwest.
The city harbors many refugees from Mexico
and the revolution. Cash registers jingle and
El Pasoans speak with unbounded enthusiasm.
By the end of the decade the population moves
up to 102,000—a fair-sized city.

By 1922, Mesa Avenue is paved all the way
from downtown to Cincinnati Street, and construction is underway on the Mesa road from
Cincinnati across seven miles of rocky arroyos to
tie up with Doniphan Drive in the Upper
Valley.

The slag dump from the old Federal Copper
Smelter was removed to make way for the building of Memorial Park, El Paso's largest. In the
early twenties Piedras Street was still unpaved,
and after heavy rains flood waters washed tons

of sand and boulders down from the east slopes of Mt. Franklin into the Five Points area.

In 1922, the town of Newman, on the Texas-New Mexico line, was officially mapped and filed. Sunrise Acres subdivision was filed in 1929 in far northeast El Paso on the Newman Road. Country Club Acres in the Upper Valley was filed in 1926. In 1928, Mayor R. E. Thomason officially dedicated El Paso's first airport.

El Pasoans danced the Charleston and went to vaudeville and movie houses like the Texas Grand, the Crawford, the Grecian, the Alhambra, the Unique, the American, the Bijou and the Wigwam. The Plaza Theater opened grandly in 1930. After the shows they flocked to an elegant ice cream parlor called the Elite Confectionery where the W. T. Grant Company is now located.

The Elite had a huge marble ice cream bar decorated with stained glass and surrounded by tables and booths. The management served up a heady selection of ice cream sodas and an ice cream concoction known as the chocolate-covered baseball.

THE new Volstead Act outlawed liquor on a national scale and the shadow of Prohibition settled across the nation. As the sources of liquor began to dry up, the eyes of Texas and other states began to focus on Juarez. Americans were looking for a drink, and they knew they could find a legal one in Mexico. Juarez put out the welcome mat along with a diversity of entertainment unequaled on the border. And now it was Juarez' turn to boom. It changed almost overnight from a sleepy little adobe town to a Mecca for fun-loving Americans. Along with the merry makers, the bootleggers came too, and they hauled vast quantities of Mexican booze in canvas-topped trucks back to Chicago and the Midwest. Hard on the heels of the bootleggers and smugglers came a new villain—the hijacker. He merely hung around the border, and when the illicit booze was delivered to the El Paso side of the Rio Grande, he moved in on the boot-

legger and relieved him of his merchandise at gunpoint. In 1921, the *El Paso Herald* reported that "mounted smugglers and Mexican river guards clashed Saturday night, 300 yards west of the eastern end of the 'island'. More than 50 shots were fired, according to the report given out yesterday by Raphael D. Avila, chief of the river guards."

RUNNING gun battles were all in a night's work for U.S. Customs agents, and seventeen of them were killed in a brief five years—between 1928 and 1933—along the Texas to Arizona strip of border.

Back across the river El Pasoans talked about an exciting new form of entertainment—radio. In 1929, Station KTSM came on the air with its first show featuring live entertainment by Karl the Kowhand — better known today as Karl Wyler, president of KTSM Radio and TV. For a short time KTSM shared facilities and air time with Station WDAH which was owned by the Methodist Church. The broadcasts emanated from the basement of Tri State Music Company, next to the Ellanay Theater on El Paso Street. The letters TSM stood for Tri State Music.

The first night football game in the Southwest was played in 1928 in El Paso High School stadium.

El Paso's skyline began to take on a brand new look in the twenties. The First National Bank building, on Sheldon Alley and Oregon, was constructed in 1921. In 1926, the Cortez Hotel, designed by architect Henry Trost, opened as the Hotel Orndorff. The following year the ownership changed and it was renamed Hotel Hussmann. Fortunately, for the changeover of the large electric sign atop the building, the names Orndorff and Hussmann both contained the same number of letters. However, the name changed again a few years later to Hotel Cortez. As the decade came to a close two other new high rise buildings were beginning to take shape —the Bassett Tower and the Hilton Hotel.

And then the Great Depression closed in.

SCENIC DRIVE was originally
known as Mountain Drive
in the early 1920's. Built partly by
chain gang labor, it was finally
paved in 1932.

PARK EMPLOYEE feeds one
of the alligators in San Jacinto Plaza
while spectators look on.
The alligators were removed from
the Plaza in the mid-1960's.

101

Evolution of a corner: West Overland and South El Paso

TWO COUSINS, Lightbody and James, seeking their fortunes on the western frontier, opened a general store on the northwest corner of West Overland and South El Paso streets in 1881. This two-story frame structure, called the Davis Block, was one of the most imposing in El Paso, and part of it remained for many years. This picture was taken from the roof of the Butterfield Stage building across South El Paso Street.

IN 1901, The Popular Dry Goods Company took over the location for its first home. The Popular was remodeled and plastered, but you will notice that the cornice at the top of the old building is still the same. Notice also part of the original building at right has become Phil Young's Cafe.

PROGRESS removed most of the old building to make way for the Grecian Theater. This picture was taken about 1918, before Phil Young's Cafe was closed by Prohibition. Note that stairs have been added from the sidewalk leading to a hotel. Also Given Brothers have moved in at far right. The picture shows the original frame structure and cornice virtually unchanged.

EXCEPT for the general shape, all recognizable features of the old Davis Block have disappeared in this 1971 photograph. The Venice Cafe and Bar have occupied this old corner since the mid-1930's. Thirman's Studio occupies the location of Phil Young's Cafe.

OPEN AIR TROLLEYS replaced El Paso's mule cars in 1902.
This picture was taken on 16th of September Street in Juarez as the trolley was passing the west corner of the Juarez Custom house.

The trolleys clanged off in all directions

During the twenties, when El Pasoans wanted to get from one point to another, they usually rode the streetcar. Automobiles were still relatively scarce—especially at the first of the decade. Most folks didn't own cars, and those who did still had to maneuver through some bone-jarring city streets. So they went by trolley, and the system worked pretty well.

El Paso's streetcar system reached its peak during the twenties, carrying passengers to all corners of the city; Fort Bliss, Government Hill, Manhattan, Washington Park, Kern Place, High School, Mesa, Highland Park, Second Ward, Smelter, and of course, Juarez.

Part of the city's original old streetcar system, the Juarez line, was still alive and well in 1971 and was carrying 10,000 to 12,000 passengers a day for the lowest fares in the nation (you can ride from Juarez to El Paso for fifteen centavos, or 1.2 cents). Today, U.S. streetcars on tracks survive only in El Paso, San Francisco, Boston, Philadelphia and Pittsburgh. El Paso's street-car line to Juarez is one of only six international trolleys in the entire world. There are two different lines running from Switzerland to France, two from Switzerland to Italy and one from Spain to France.

As the use of trolleys began to decline all over the country, El Paso's transportation styles also changed. Some buses were put into service in 1926, and in 1929 buses replaced the familiar little trolley on the Smelter line. In 1937, a great majority of the streetcars were abandoned, and by 1940 all of the old trolley lines had been converted to buses with the exception of Fort Bliss, Washington Park and Juarez lines. By 1950, only the Juarez line was left, and El Paso City Lines began using a much newer trolley, called the PCC car. These were imported from San Diego when that city finally abandoned the use of streetcars. El Paso's streetcars still furnish a visual link with the romance of past years as well as providing needed transportation between two border cities.

LATER MODEL CARS kept passengers out of the weather. Here the Depot trolley picks up a customer in Pioneer Plaza. At right is the Sheldon Hotel. The present Mills Building was not yet built when this picture was taken.

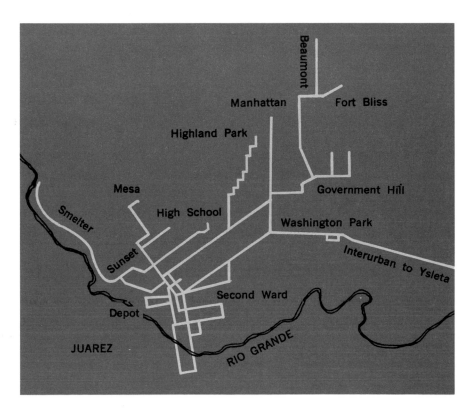

MAP SHOWS El Paso streetcar lines that covered the city during the mid-twenties.

BIG CLANGING CARS like this one on the Fort Bliss line lasted until 1947. Until then, the big cars were still running to Washington Park and Juarez as well as to Fort Bliss. This picture was taken during World War II just after the streetcar passed under the railroad viaduct on Copia Street.

SMALL, four-wheeled "Birney" cars served El Paso's growing neighborhoods into the late 1930's. At top is the Manhattan trolley in 1930. The bottom picture shows the Mesa car on its last day of existence in February, 1938 at its stop in Madeline Park. The Mesa cars went up North Oregon Street, then east of Dudley School to Kern Place. The fare was six cents for adults, three cents for children.

STORMSVILLE was a settlement on the mesa after the Rio Grande flood of 1897 dissolved adobe houses in the lower parts of town. The dirt road in the foreground is now Rim Road, and the adobe houses (above) gave way in the late 1920's to some of the city's finest residences.

TEXAS GRAND Theater provided El Pasoans with top-quality vaudeville when this picture was taken in 1925. The site is now an El Paso Natural Gas Company parking lot at Texas and Campbell streets.

HARRY MITCHELL'S Mint Cafe was famous for its "New Orleans Gin Fizz."
Like most of the other popular bars, it was located on 16th of September Street near the Lerdo
corner. Note the slot machines and brass spittoons for tobacco chewers.

¡ Salud!

During prohibition days El Pasoans, as well as famous visitors from all over the country, enjoyed the cultural centers of Juarez. On Saturday nights the streets of Juarez bulged with the generation of the twenties. And the fun centered around 16th of September Street and Lerdo where business boomed in spots like the Big Kid's, The Tivoli, Harry Mitchell's Mint Bar, the O.K. Bar, and the old Central Cafe. Guest books and pictures signed by celebrities visiting the Mint and the Central read like a Who's Who of entertainers, politicians and sportsmen of the twenties. Among the famous were Jack Dempsey, Jim Jeffries, Eddie Rickenbacker, Amelia Earhart, H. L. Mencken and Mayor Jimmie Walker of New York.

Another flourishing spot, although not nearly as first class, was an adobe saloon called the Hole in the Wall. Its location alone was enough to keep it crowded for a number of years during prohibition. The Hole in the Wall was on Cordova Island west of where the foot of Piedras Street meets Paisano Drive today. Its clientele didn't bother with such formalities as U.S. Customs inspections; they merely parked their cars, lifted the wire fence and walked across a plank which served as a foot bridge over an irrigation ditch. After a rain, people's feet got a bit muddy but they didn't seem to mind. After all, here they were living it up in adobe splendor and having mixed drinks within a few feet of the dry old U.S.A.

On the American side, one of the favorite eating spots was the Modern Cafe, located in the basement of the Mills Building. The Modern had a dance floor and dinner music combined with jazzy elegance that appealed to El Paso tastes during the roaring twenties.

THE TIVOLI was a wide-open gambling casino during Prohibition.

16TH OF SEPTEMBER Street was Juarez's fun center.

CENTRAL CAFE at Lerdo and
16th of September streets was
a favorite spot for celebrities visiting
the border as well as for
thirsty El Pasoans.

109

COLLEGE OF MINES looked
lonesome out among the rocks in
1921. Enrollment that year
reached 106 shortly after the name
was changed from Texas State
School of Mines.

FEW PARKING problems were
encountered by students who drove
tin lizzies over unpaved
campus streets. Cars at right
are parked in front of what is now
known as "Old Main."

CLOCHE HATS topped the
heads of 1929's fashion-minded
women. They also wore
dresses such as these advertised in
the El Paso Evening Post.

W. T. GRANT CO.
Style Apparel Section
The MARLEN Shop

at GRANT'S

these print and flat crepe Summer Frocks
again prove that style can be inexpensive

A five-dollar bill that once wouldn't even buy a hat will bring
you one of these smart, washable crepe dresses in soft pastel
colorings.

The print dresses come in Navy and White dots
and other Summer patterns.

$5

The styles
include plaited
circular skirts,
Bolero jackets
and tailored
sport models
in sizes
14 to 48

Like all Grant
merchandise
these dresses are
guaranteed

GRANT'S
Ready to Wear
Featuring Style and Economy

Your purchase
price will be
refunded
if they fail
to satisfy

MESA AT TEXAS

111

FORT BLISS blimp hanger was a major El Paso landmark for many years. It was built in 1919 and torn down in 1955.

THIS FORMATION of DH-4 airplanes was part of a review for General Pershing's triumphal return to Fort Bliss in 1920. The picture was taken from a spot about where the Fort Bliss polo field is located. In the background at left is Sugarloaf Peak.

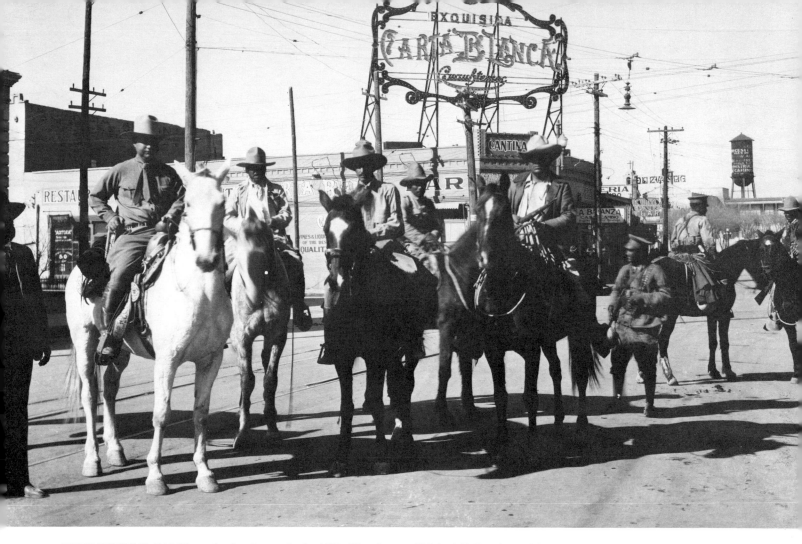

REVOLUTION CAME to the border again in 1929. The Juarez Chief of Police (on white horse) discusses imminent attack on Juarez with mounted troops.

1929: the Escobar Revolution

Fort Bliss Troops were called to battle stations along the river once again in 1929 when another revolution broke out in Mexico. This was the Escobar Revolution, led by General Jose Escobar, and for awhile it looked like the old days all over again. Rebel troops came up from the south and made preparations for the inevitable attack on Juarez, the most important city in the north. American 1st Cavalry Division troopers under General George Moseley went into action. They quickly threw up sandbag barricades near the bridges between Stanton and Santa Fe streets, preparing to defend American soil if necessary.

And just like the old days of the Madero Rev-

olution, El Pasoans thronged high spots like the First National Bank Building to get a view of the fighting. But the battle for Juarez lasted less than a day. One American citizen was killed, although rifle bullets thudded into a number of buildings in downtown El Paso. General Moseley himself went to Juarez and persuaded the commander of the Juarez garrison to surrender the city. The rebels won this round, secured the city of Juarez, and once again Fort Bliss troops pulled out of south El Paso. Little more than a month later, however, the rebel cause withered and died, and peace settled once again on Juarez and El Paso.

The silent flickers

Much like commercials on today's television programs, the silent movie houses of the 1920's had their messages between reels. The glass slides on these two pages are a few of hundreds that were found reposing in the basement of the State Theater.

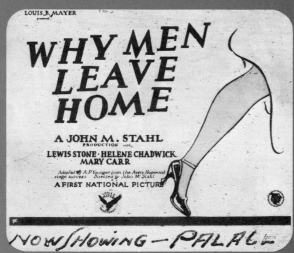

HILTON HOTEL (now the
Plaza Hotel) under construction
looked like this in July, 1930.
It was built by R. E. McKee on the
site of the old Sheldon Hotel
which burned down in 1929.

seven

The
lean
years

A short 50 years witnesses the transformation of the old adobe settlement at the Pass to a modern city of more than a hundred thousand people. Before 1929, people make fortunes gambling that El Paso sand dunes would someday be worth considerably more than fifty dollars an acre. Most El Pasoans know poverty only by reputation. But in October, 1929, the bottom drops out of the stock market and it's hard to believe that the bubble has burst. But it has — and everything grinds to a halt. The boom is all over and it is going to take cool heads to journey through the years ahead. This is the hard times generation.

The stock market crash plunged the country and most of the world into the worst economic crisis in history, and its first effects were felt in El Paso by the beginning of the new decade of 1930.

As the Depression deepened, the thirties brought about the lowest ebb in El Paso's growth. Construction on the Hilton Hotel and the Bassett Tower, which started during 1929, was completed in 1930, but it was almost two decades before anything resembling the activity of previous years was to start again at the Pass. Around the country hourly wages had dropped sixty percent since 1929. Farmers were getting five cents a pound for cotton. The number of unemployed rose to a record 25 percent of the labor force.

The *El Paso Herald* was sold to *The Post* and became the *El Paso Herald-Post*. In 1931, the First National Bank failed. The relief rolls swelled. In the mid-thirties, you could get a full course dinner at Waters' Cafe on the corner of Texas and Kansas for fifteen cents. These were the dark days of the WPA, the NRA, and the CCC. And Highway 80 going west was filled with rattletrap cars heading for California from the dust bowl of Texas and Oklahoma.

But in El Paso all was not poverty and defeat. A whole generation of young El Pasoans grew up during the thirties without even knowing

117

times were that tough. They went to school and put pieces of cardboard in the bottom of their shoes so the holes in the soles wouldn't show so badly. They didn't have any money to spend and they couldn't get jobs. But they didn't know any better, and they had fun growing up in those quiet, hard times. To them, El Paso was just the same old place they had remembered from infancy. The town looked just the same for twenty years. There were so few new houses being built it was an occasion worthy of a Sunday afternoon drive to see a house under construction. In 1933, only eight homes were built in El Paso. There were three public high schools, El Paso, Austin and Bowie. And Ysleta, that county school way down the valley. El Paso High was still known to most people as "High School". Even printed football programs from Austin announced that their Panthers were playing "High School".

IT was an innocent age when teenagers (they weren't even called that yet) went to movies at the Ellanay and the Wigwam and the Palace and the Plaza and then hung around the Five Points Oasis or the Old Town Pump. Or the Spinning Wheel on Montana Street which advertised giant sized malts in every flavor from avocado to pistachio. As a year-end salute to El Paso's mid-winter sun, a post-season football game was staged in 1935 between a team composed of El Paso high school all-stars and the Ranger, Texas, high school football team. This was to be the first Sun Bowl Game. The idea caught on and the performance was repeated the following year, but with college teams. With the addition of other events, including a parade with bands and colorful floats, the overall project was dubbed "Sun Carnival." The Carnival launched a queen for the first time. Civic organizations promoted duchesses and the tradition was carried on in much the same manner—with sophisticated changes — even through the war years and continues in popularity.

In the mid-thirties the Sunday afternoon drive was a high point for middle-class families. The route usually took people down the North Loop Road under the leafy canopy formed by the huge old cottonwoods that lined both sides of the road. Then if the kids behaved, they stopped at Hazel Barner's Candy Shop or maybe at Price's Dairy in Five Points for an ice cream cone. A more spectacular family treat was out Doniphan Drive where people parked their cars after sundown and watched spellbound as smelter workers dumped whole trainloads of glowing red slag down the mountains.

In 1938, El Pasoans listened on radio to Gangbusters, Charlie McCarthy, Rudy Valle, Burns and Allen, Amos 'n' Andy, Fibber McGee and Molly, Bing Crosby, Jimmy Fiddler's Hollywood Gossip, Kay Kayser's College of Musical Knowledge, and the Green Hornet. Sunday nights were usually reserved for Jack Benny, the Manhattan Merry-Go-Round, and the Hour of Charm with Phil Spitalny's All Girl Orchestra. In 1936, Dorrance Roderick, publisher of *The El Paso Times,* applied to the FCC for permission to operate a radio station in El Paso and it went on the air in 1940, under the call letters KROD.

Not nearly as in keeping with this age of innocence was El Paso's red light district. As late as 1937 organized prostitution was wide open in an area which centered on Ninth Street and Mesa Avenue. The Silver Dollar Bar was a swinging spot at all hours and even at midnight the lights were so bright in the so-called "zone of tolerance" it could pass for high noon.

THE supercharged momentum built up by the nation's economy during the twenties was not stopped completely short by the Depression. Although El Paso coasted downhill through the early thirties, the enthusiasm which could sweep the city for a new fad was still prevalent, but the tendency was to something inexpensive; miniature golf, dance marathons, bank night, pin ball machines and chain letters. And Mitchell's Premium Beer. All over the country, PWA employees were leaning on shovels. Later, a freshman at Harvard gulped down a goldfish on a bet and started a fad which didn't end until 1938 when someone downed 42 in succession. Goldfish gulping tests were also very big at the College of Mines, and El Paso's big bands, Jimmie Fields' Orchestra and The Varsitonians, played "Stardust" and "Deep Purple" and "Body and Soul" and the rest of the sweet swing of the thirties.

The college crowds packed Tom Burchell's Bar that straddled the Texas-New Mexico state line. And in Juarez they frequented the Rio Grande Bar where they drank tequila almondrada, sweet soda and lime and bought steak sandwiches for fifteen cents or a full steak dinner for thirty-five. But prices were still pretty low on the American side. At a little diner called Pop's Place next door to the Hotel Cortez, you could get two hamburgers, a pint of Price's milk and a fourth of a large pie (any flavor) for twenty-five cents.

In 1939, Hitler invaded Poland, and the world —at least in Europe—burst into flames for the second time in a generation. In the United States the big thing was "preparedness" and the defense factories boomed. The Oakies and Arkies and Texans moved in a steady stream through El Paso on U.S. 80 to pick prunes or work in southern California's aircraft plants. And, in 1940, the Census Bureau showed El Paso's population to be 98,000 — a drop of 4,000 since 1930. It had been a rough decade.

BUT the war still seemed a long way off to El Pasoans until that particular December seventh in 1941 when they found out they, too, were at war — and doing badly.

At the beginning of World War II Fort Bliss was the largest cavalry post in the United States, but by 1943 the post was rapidly becoming an anti-aircraft artillery post. The old Union Depot downtown took on new life as it was thronged with thousands of people every day. Countless troop trains moved in and out of El Paso. El Paso women helped raise funds for a good cause —Bundles for Britain. They held a weekly luncheon at the old Turney home (now the El Paso Museum of Art), with sorority girls from the College of Mines serving food.

IN 1944, history's greatest invasion force landed in Normandy. The 1st Cavalry Division waded ashore in the Philippines and was first to reenter Manila. Germany surrendered in 1945 and after the A-bomb dropped on Hiroshima and Nagasaki, Japan followed suit. 1st Cavalry troops were the first Americans to enter Tokyo.

With the end of the war businessmen were free once more to go after the markets and pent-up demand which years of wartime restrictions had built up. Veterans began returning to El Paso by the thousands. The first year after the war, fall registration at the College of Mines jumped from a wartime enrollment of 765 to 1,764. A new bank opened — The Southwest National. New housing was needed badly all over the city, and for the first time in many years El Pasoans were to watch new subdivisions springing up. The first was Loretto Place, in 1946. The developer, Bill Mayfield and a family team, started Loretto No. 1 with forty acres of sandhills — twenty more than he really felt he could use. But Loretto set the pace and style for all the others to follow. It was El Paso's first subdivision to be built without alleys. It was also the first area since Kern Place to be designed on a curvilinear plan. In 1948, Loretto Shopping Center became El Paso's pioneer suburban center, put together in a piecemeal fashion without much provision for parking (since few people knew much about shopping centers). It violated every rule in the book—but then the book hadn't been written yet. Everybody learned something from Loretto. Shortly afterward came Loretto No. 2 and No. 3, and the original forty acres grew to 120. Terry Allen subdivision was filed in 1947, and there were many more to come. The decade of the fifties was to turn little El Paso into a major city.

The stage was set for spectacular expansion.

TEAMS OF HORSES and
mules provided muscle for digging
the foundation of the Bassett Tower.
R. E. McKee was the contractor.

RED BRICK Federal Courthouse
was still part of El Paso's skyline in
February, 1930. In the foreground
construction of the Hilton Hotel
is in early stages.

BASSETT TOWER exterior nears completion on February 1, 1930. Only four and
a half months elapsed between the time this picture was taken and the start of the building on
the page at left.

EL PASOANS gathered to see the arrival of the first airplane at Municipal Airport on a regular service schedule. Standard Airlines was later taken over by Western Air Express between El Paso and Los Angeles. It later became American Airlines.

SUNDAY DRIVES were calm and peaceful under the bower of big cottonwoods in the lower valley. This picture was taken in 1931 on U.S. 80.

KERN PLACE, even in 1930, was pretty isolated from the rest of El Paso. The Mesa Road is in the foreground, intersecting with wide Cincinnati Street at lower right.

AUSTIN HIGH SCHOOL takes shape in mid-1930.
This is one of many El Paso buildings constructed by R. E. McKee.

KIDD FIELD and Holiday Hall on the College of Mines campus were built in the early thirties by WPA labor. The football game crowd (above) didn't quite fill the new stadium when the picture was taken in 1933. By the mid-thirties (below) the College of Mines had paved streets and enrollment edged up toward 1,000.

TEENAGERS of the thirties and forties will remember one of their favorite hangouts, the Five Points Oasis. Maybe it just *seemed* bigger and more glamorous than this 1937 picture would seem to indicate. This is now the parking lot for the Empire Club.

AUSTIN HIGH students dedicated their new stadium in 1936.

SAN JACINTO PLAZA in the late thirties had trees so thick, it had a jungle-like appearance from across Main Street where this picture was taken.

RUBBERNECK BUS tours of El Paso and Juarez left from Camp Grande on Alameda Street. This forerunner of motor hotels claimed to be the first in the United States.

DOME of the old City Hall sticks up above the trees in this 1936 photograph. Note the Park streetcar at left and the County Court House before it was remodeled many years later.

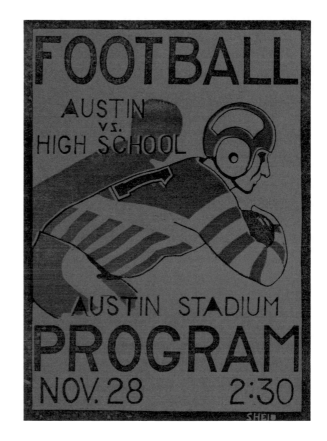

FOOTBALL
AUSTIN
vs.
HIGH SCHOOL

AUSTIN STADIUM
PROGRAM
NOV. 28   2:30

EL PASO HIGH and Austin students turned out en masse for their annual Thanksgiving Day football game. Note that this program, for the 1936 game, still used the name "High School" to designate El Paso High.

MISS FORD V-8 added a touch of glamour to El Paso in 1935. Pan American Airways' Ford Tri-motor plane in the background was the latest in deluxe passenger comfort.

TRAFFIC was light in 1935 along Juarez Avenue and you could get a steak dinner for thirty-five cents. This picture was taken looking south from the Santa Fe Street bridge.

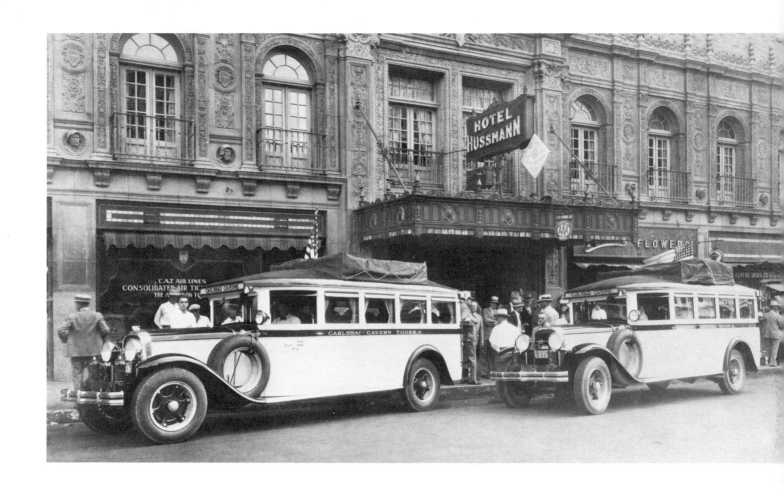

Pork Shoulder Roast (U.S. Inspected)
Shank End—Per Pound_____ **13c**
Ham—Armours—Fixed Flavor—
Half or Whole—Per Pound____ **22½c**
Hamburger—Per Pound, 10c;
3 Pounds for_____ **25c**
Beef Chuck Roast—
Per pound _____ **9c**
Beef Round or Sirloin Steak—
Per Pound _____ **20c**
Hens, Small, Fresh Killed—
Per pound _____ **22c**
Roast Veal Shoulder—
Per pound _____ **11c**
Beef or Veal Stew Meat—
Per Pound _____ **6c**
Pork Chops—(U. S. Inspected)
End Cuts—Per Pound_____ **18c**
Roast Pork Loin (U. S, Inspected)
End Cuts—Per Pound_____ **18c**
Pig Liver
Per Pound _____ **10c**

CLARENCE SAUNDERS
SOLE OWNER OF MY NAME

LONG-NOSED buses load passengers in front of Hotel Hussmann for the inaugural trip to Carlsbad Caverns in 1930.

LOW FOOD PRICES during the Depression may be remembered longingly by some El Pasoans. This grocery ad by Clarence Saunders stores appeared in the Labor Advocate of June 12, 1931.

The horse soldiers: Fort Bliss was home base

THE LAST of the "Old" Army played out its role in the Fort Bliss of the late 1930's and early 1940's. Fort Bliss was home of the 1st Cavalry Division and the romantic era of the horse soldiers lasted until 1943.

SIX-FOOT RATTLESNAKE was no match for troopers of the 1st Cavalry at Fort Bliss.

HORSE-DRAWN ARTILLERY passes in review at Fort Bliss in the early forties.

This big yellow and black shoulder patch was a familiar sight on El Paso streets until the 1st Cavalry became mechanized and turned in their horses in 1943.

FIELD ARTILLERY had plenty of space to maneuver at Fort Bliss, the largest cavalry post in the U.S.

TEEN CANTEEN, an El Paso youth center was opened up by Vernus Carey and the YMCA during World War II.

The wartime teenagers

In spite of World War II, gasoline rationing, and a hometown full of soldiers, life went on for the local kids. In 1944, the YMCA's Vernus Carey opened up a youth center called the Teen Canteen in the old Jewish Temple on Oregon Street. Teenagers jitterbugged to a loud jukebox playing wartime favorites by Benny Goodman, Tommy Dorsey and Glenn Miller. They also drank thousands of Cokes and puffed an occasional cigarette outside and because of the scarcity of gasoline they usually double and

triple dated. Some of them were even known to carry an "Oklahoma Credit Card" — a short length of garden hose to be used just in case they ran out of gas and had to help themselves to somebody else's.

Aside from liberating a little gasoline once in a while, 1940's teenagers in El Paso were pretty much like their predecessors of the thirties. They didn't demonstrate or riot, and in those hectic times they considered themselves lucky to be eating mom's—or anyone's—apple pie.

HEADQUARTERS of the Teen Canteen during World War II was the old Jewish temple at the corner of Oregon Street and Yandell Boulevard. This picture was taken in the early 1940's, just before the Teen Canteen moved in.

SAN JACINTO PLAZA had a verdant look in the late 1940's.

SHOPPING CENTERS, usually
surrounded by sprawling subdivisions,
mushroomed during the fifties.

eight

The fast-changing fifties

THE fabulous fifties change El Paso from a nice little town into a bustling city. It is like the good old days all over again, and El Paso's population more than doubles — from 130,000 in 1950 to 276,000 in 1960.

The chemistry that causes the change evolves from a mixture of many elements; the post war rush to furnish long-awaited luxuries, a general westward migration of Americans—particularly Midwesterners coming to the Southwest for a gentler climate, and a new affluence; a jingling of coins in one's jeans after so many years of budgeting and rationing. Also, federal agencies like the FHA and VA making it possible for the great American public to buy homes on low down payment installment plans.

But still, no one dreams of what is really getting ready to happen.

Military spending started building up again when, in June, 1950, North Korean troops invaded South Korea and the U.S. entered a new war with Douglas McArthur in command of its forces. Fort Bliss expanded its establishments and built new ones. The construction trades in El Paso boomed, and civilian and military employment increased steadily in El Paso, Las Cruces and Alamogordo.

BY the early fifties, the areas inside El Paso's city limits were developed and settled, and people began moving outside the city. The cactus-covered rocky slopes on the west side of the city began to take on a new luster. When the first Mission Hills subdivision was filed in 1951, it was outside the city limits. Then came Marwood and Westwood in 1953. In 1954, the city annexed 25 square miles of land which make up the present Upper Valley. Piedmont Hills was filed in 1953, and Coronado Hills came along in 1955, followed by Crown Point the same year. Coronado was so far out of town and so quiet, one housewife quipped that the most exciting thing to do on Saturday night was to go up to the new Minute Market and count the cans. In 1957, Ridgecrest, Crestmont and Coronado Country Club Estates were filed, and in 1959, came Coronado Country Club Foothills and Coronado Terrace.

In 1950, the population of northeast El Paso was officially 201. Within five years it jumped to 8,800, and by 1959 it was more than 29,000. Building construction was moving so fast, even native El Pasoans were complaining of getting lost in their own home town. In 1953, the city annexed 11 square miles of land on the north side of the Logan Heights cantonment that moved the city limits more than six miles north. The newly-annexed area added about 8,000 residents to the population. At the edge of town in 1953, the Mountain View subdivision plat was filed. Park Foothills was filed in 1954, and in the next year came Milagro Hills. Milagro means "miracle" in Spanish. And that's what most people figured; the area was so far away from anything, it would be a miracle if anybody

bought a lot and moved out there. And the red sand desert east of the Franklins began to sprout housing developments at an unbelievable rate; Monterrey Hills and Colonia Verde, followed by Dolphin Terrace and Sun Valley, and many others until northeast El Paso became almost a new city.

El Pasoans moved to their new subdivisions, mowed new lawns, drank an occasional beer, and burned a thousand steaks in their backyards.

Down the valley came Clardy Fox, Lakeside, Hacienda Heights, Ranchland Hills and Loma Terrace. In 1955, the city officially annexed 44 square miles of the Lower Valley, and the old town of Ysleta became a part of El Paso. Any resemblance of El Paso of the fifties to that of any previous decade was, as they say, purely coincidental.

Out Montana Street, bulldozers pushed the sand away and plats were filed for Zia Village, Cielo Vista, Valley View, Scottsdale and Eastwood.

SOUTH El Paso, as had been the case for years, was generally ignored by all the new building and expanding and affluence. The two story tenement houses were still crowded with human beings. This was the most densely populated part of the city, yet it was the most neglected. Twenty-five years earlier, the famous Kessler Report had strongly recommended that the city should "proceed with the sanitation of Chihuahuita (as South El Paso was called) and have a thorough cleaning up in the sections where human habitations are congested . . . This entire district instead of being an eyesore, unhealthful and a disgrace to the city, can be and ought to be made a section of exotic charm and special interest to visitors and residents. Community centers and great vocational schools are needed here."

But a modest start was made in the early fifties with the construction of Tays, Paisano and Sherman Place housing projects. In 1958, civic leaders and city government convened to begin programs seeking general community improvement.

MOST El Pasoans were able to look beyond the problems brought about by the fast changing fifties and they enjoyed the cultural wonders of this brave new world. An outlandish spring rite called "cramming" swept college campuses in the late fifties, and at Texas Western College (the new name acquired by the College of Mines in 1949)students crammed about twenty of their peers into a phone booth, and even more into a Volkswagen. Colorful plastic rings called hula hoops kept El Paso kids busy gyrating and El Paso doctors busy treating their parents for sacroiliac problems.

A new face appeared one night at the El Paso Coliseum—a kid with long sideburns and some strange-sounding new music that he pounded out on a guitar. His name was Elvis Presley. In the meantime, KROD-TV came on the air as El Paso's pioneer television station in late December, 1952. Across the city, KTSM-TV officially came on the video tube in January, 1953, and El Pasoans raved about Milton Berle and sat in darkened rooms watching nine-inch screens. Everybody loved Lucy. They stayed glued to their screens to watch The Jackie Gleason Show, Dinah Shore, Our Miss Brooks, Phil Silvers, Davy Crockett, and the Mickey Mouse Club. On Saturday nights Sid Caesar's Show of Shows held top ratings until it died of exposure. It was an era of q u i z shows, and a program called What's My Line outlasted them all. KELP-TV came on the air in 1956. In Juarez, possibly because of television, big, brassy night clubs like the Tivoli, the Lobby No. 2, the Charmont and the Chinese Palace were beginning to die in the early fifties. But many people still remember the immortal words of Johnny Armendariz, MC at the Chinese Palace, when he opened each show of the evening with: "Good evening ladies and gentlemen, welcome to the Chinese Palace, the noisiest little gin mill on the border!" Or come-

dian Eddie Lane with his you-all lines like: "Oh hail yes!" or "You dyam right!". Later in the decade, a baroque nightclub called La Fiesta was billed as the "most beautiful in the Americas", and for the first time in years the border was attracting top names in the entertainment world like the Kingston Trio, Earl Grant and the Ames Brothers. The strip joints along Juarez Avenue packed them in on Saturday nights and mariachi music blared out into the streets from dozens of bars.

After almost a quarter of a century, even the face of downtown El Paso began to change. El Paso Natural Gas Company moved into its new eighteen-story home office building in 1955. And in spite of the bright new shopping centers popping up on the outskirts of the city, downtown El Paso never saw empty store fronts and boarded-up buildings as did many large cities all over the country during this great age of the shopping center. In 1950, Mayor Dan Duke drove the first train through the new Bataan Memorial Trainway, a long-needed project that put the railroad tracks below the surface through the downtown district. The new public library was completed in 1954.

Not to be outdone by El Paso, Texas Western College put on a building boom of its own. Sticking closely to the original Bhutanese architecture, they built Magoffin Auditorium, the Biology Building, Miner's Hall, the Women's Gym, and a new Administration Building.

IT had been a great decade for the city at the Pass. Its city limits, by 1959 zoomed to 114 square miles—quite a contrast to only 29 square miles in 1950. The old feel of confidence was back in the air and people from all over the country came to El Paso to buy a piece of the action. Many of them got rich in the process, and many El Pasoans sat there and watched it happen and quietly cursed themselves for not buying up northeast El Paso when it could have been bought so cheaply such a short time before.

FOR SEVENTY YEARS the railroads moved at street level through the heart of El Paso. This picture shows a long freight train moving through the city shortly before the tracks were depressed in 1950.

The Bataan Trainway becomes a reality in 1950

BIG SOUTHERN PACIFIC locomotive heads for the center of El Paso. Construction on track depression is underway at left center of picture.

TRAINWAY PROJECT moves into high gear in this picture, looking west from Stanton Street. In 1950, Mayor Dan Duke, an **ex-railroader**, drove the first train through the new Bataan Memorial Trainway.

EL PASO NATURAL GAS Company made the first major addition to El Paso's skyline in two decades when it built an eighteen-story home office building in 1954.

El Pasoans moved to the outskirts
and got lost in their own hometown

MERELY TYPICAL is this aerial view of northeast El Paso growth during the fifties.
At top center is El Paso Natural Gas Company's No. 3 Compressor Station, built during the 1930's
way out in the desert, miles from anything.

SHOPPING CENTERS like Sunrise provided a new way of life for El Pasoans.

THE MT. FRANKLIN Yacht Club, a group dedicated to exploring the mountain, was active in the 1950's. This picture was taken on one of their treks and shows greenery in the Mundy's Spring area on the east side of Mt. Franklin.

EL PASO'S skyline looked like this in 1954 when El Paso Natural Gas Company's building was half completed. The other tallest buildings in El Paso included (from left) the Bassett Tower, First National Building, Hilton Hotel, Mills Building and Cortez Hotel.

HIGH ON THE EAST slopes of Mt. Franklin, Mountain Park introduced a proper desert life style for homeowners.

Mountain Park: how to get along with the environment

Long-time El Paso residents may remember a huge billboard way out north of town on the Newman Road. Its outstanding feature was a red arrow made out of a telephone pole pointing to a message which extolled the virtues of Sunrise Acres. Lots were cheap and you could buy one for ten dollars down. But, unfortunately, very few people did. The owner of Sunrise Acres was a dreamer of a man named Edgar Park. He sat out there for thirty years waiting for customers, but about the only thing that happened was that his sign faded a little more each year. Edgar Park was just ahead of his time. He thought big, and one of his dreams was to convince the government to construct a massive aqueduct to bring water from the Rio Grande across the Franklin Mountains and turn the desert green in northeast El Paso.

By the mid-fifties, however, he had sold a large part of Sunrise Acres to developers for Park Foothills subdivision. About this time developer Bill Mayfield was looking at an old survey map of the Franklin Mountains. The map showed a large area (about a mile west of Dyer Street) to be relatively flat, although visually the mountains seemed rather steep. It was adjacent to the western edge of the old Sunrise Acres property. Mayfield decided to take a personal look, so with map in hand he climbed the first big rise in the foothills. And sure enough, his map was correct; there were several hundred acres at this elevation crying to be developed. He bought the land for an average price of $375 an acre and in 1955 he filed the plat for what was to soon become Mountain Park, an unusual subdivision. Mountain Park made use of the terrain. The mountain was not bulldozed to make room for homes; the streets and homes were designed to fit the mountain. Natural desert vegetation was used in landscaping to produce a group of homes overlooking what seemed like half of West Texas, New Mexico and Chihuahua. It was the first major subdivision in the Southwest to put the electric and telephone utility wires underground. Here was a truly innovative development that made peace with the desert and the mountain and used them to the advantage of everybody.

THREE ALLIGATORS in Plaza pond were always fun to watch.

LOOKING SOUTH at the intersection of San Francisco and South El Paso streets, has been a favorite spot for photographers since the early 1880's. This picture was made in the early 1950's and shows the Ellanay Theater at right, now known as the Capri. The Ellanay was named for the initials of two men named Louis and Andreas.

EL PASO CITY HALL was
razed in 1959, and is now the site of
a small park bounded by San
Antonio and Myrtle streets.
Inset shows City Hall shortly before
demolition started.

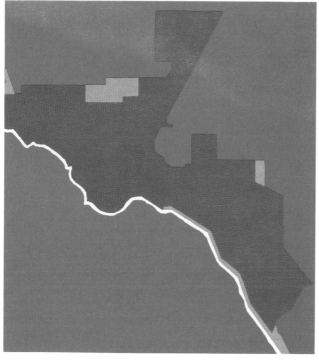

CITY LIMITS expanded wildly
during the 1950's. By 1959,
they included 114 square miles,
making El Paso one of the largest
cities in area in the United States.

Dallas St
EXIT 1 9/10 MI
80 BUSINESS 85
Downtown
EXIT 1/2 MI
Porfirio Diaz
W. Main Dr
STOP AHEAD
STOP AHEAD

EL PASO'S close tie with Mexico
is evident in this picture showing the
towers of the Juarez Mission
framed by Porfirio Diaz off-ramp
sign on Interstate 10. This
freeway through El Paso County was
completed in 1970.

nine

El Paso
grows up

NEW Year's Day 1963 dawns bright and
clear and cold as El Pasoans bundle up
to watch the Sun Carnival Parade. The afternoon before, in the sparkling new 30,000-seat
Sun Bowl, Oregon batters SMU 21 to 14 in
warm sunshine. The old pueblo at the Pass sets
the stage for bigger and better things, as it seems
like the momentum of the fifties will just keep
on going. El Paso is destined to grow to 325,000
people by 1970 and Juarez across the river is
to outstrip El Paso with a population of 500,000.

In March, 1960, *The El Paso Times* carried
an eight column b a n n e r headline that read:
"Downtown Freeway Receives Final OK". *The
Times* also mentioned that "it will take many
months to prepare maps of the route west from
Piedras Street . . . and the first land purchase

will be made next year. Actual construction of the downtown section still is a number of years off, and no downtown buildings will be torn down for at least five years." Some El Pasoans were opposed to bringing the freeway into the downtown area, and realtor Otis Coles suggested the construction of a double-deck or two-story freeway to run a b o v e the length of Paisano Drive. El Paso's first Mexican-American mayor, Raymond Telles, said that any information to support claims that the two-story freeway would be feasible and reduce costs should be presented to the State Highway Department. The actual route chosen paralleled Missouri Street through the city, and it wasn't until 1970 that El Paso's freeway w a s completed from one end of the county to the other. Also completed and opened to traffic in 1970 was the long-awaited Trans-Mountain Road across the Franklins. This connected northeast and northwest El Paso for the first time across a saddle in the mountains that caused the Texas Highway Department to blast the deepest cut in State history.

THE basketball team at Texas Western College brought instant fame to the school and the city in 1966 when it surprised the sports world by defeating the University of Kentucky for the national championship. A few months later the University of Texas Regents officially changed the name of the school to the University of Texas at El Paso. By 1971, enrollment reached almost 12,000.

The downtown skyline continued to change rapidly: In 1962, the El Paso National Bank moved into its new twenty-story building. Two years later, the Southwest National erected its bank and office building along with a Downtowner Hotel. Mutual Federal built a handsome structure at Texas and Kansas in 1967, followed by the seventeen-story Holiday Inn and the Travelodge in 1970. The State National Bank built its twenty-two-story tower in 1971, making it the tallest building in the city. But all the high rises didn't stop downtown. Out Mesa Avenue

in the Coronado area stands the highest office structure above sea level in Texas—Coronado Tower—and on the eastside near Bassett Shopping Center, the Surety Tower was opened and became a landmark in east El Paso.

It was the age of the Vietnam War and commitment and the Beatles and flower children. El Paso even fostered its first real live hippie and an occasional love-in sometime after 1967 when the Haight Ashbury epicenter began to decline. The Vietnam War placed added demands on Fort Bliss, but things were a lot different now at the old cavalry post. The fort had become the largest air defense center in the free world and occupied a million acres, a greater land area than the State of Rhode Island. Desert land within the city limits continued to fill up briskly with subdivisions although it was not like the frantic pace of the fifties. In 1960 Thunderbird Valley and Fiesta Hills were filed on the westside. Lomas del Rey was filed in 1961. In northeast El Paso came Sun Valley in 1960, Park North in 1966, and on the eastside, Vista Del Sol in 1968.

El Paso's cool teenage girls wore miniskirts and hotpants. Long hair styles for boys reached to the shoulders of many and created disputes on morality that will probably never be settled. Teenagers didn't worry any more about a place to hang out like they did in the good old days of the Teen Canteen. It was the age of the drive-in food franchise, and they could literally drive for miles on Montana Street or Dyer or Mesa and never be more than thirty seconds from a roast beef sandwich or a pizza, or a hamburger or fried chicken.

EL PASOANS — starting in 1971 — could finally order a legal cocktail from a public bar. In 1971, Texas changed its liquor laws that had dried up the entire state since prohibition days a half-century before. Now El Pasoans no longer had to carry a bottle in a brown paper sack when they attended formal dances and parties.

AERIAL TRAMWAY carries passengers to mile-high Ranger Peak for a view of three states in two nations. Attractive motor hotels like the one below built during the 1960's create a resort atmosphere for El Paso.

THE UNIVERSITY OF TEXAS at El Paso became the new name for Texas Western College in 1966.

U.T. EL PASO campus, as it begins the 1970's, is a far cry from the lonely buildings out in the rocks during the early twenties.

STUDENT ENROLLMENT reached almost 12,000 in 1971.

The Plaza changeth

MOST FOLKS, it seems, want to take a crack at landscaping San Jacinto Plaza. Palms were planted in the late 1950's.

IN 1961, the Plaza looked like this with a few of the big old elm trees remaining. Alligators still sunned themselves in center pool.

IN THE MID-SIXTIES the Plaza fronting Mills Street added plastic-roofed seating areas for bus riders.

IN 1969, they started all over again. This picture was made from atop the Mills Building looking east.

SAN JACINTO PLAZA in 1971 was beginning to look more like its old self, but still had a long way to go.

153

U. S. PRESIDENT Lyndon Johnson and Mexico's president Gustavo Diaz Ordaz meet to officially mark the Chamizal settlement.

ON CUE, the Rio Grande flows deep and full in its new channel as crowds watch the official Chamizal settlement ceremonies from atop international bridge.

BOWIE HIGH SCHOOL'S football team practices in spite of the Border Highway construction going on in the background during 1971. The overpass is part of the project resulting from the Chamizal settlement.

El Chamizal: the fence gets mended

On a warm dusty October day in 1967 two heads of state met in El Paso and Juarez to mend the fence separating the two countries. This was the ceremony marking the solution of the century-old Chamizal boundary dispute between the United States and Mexico.

United States President Lyndon Johnson and Mexico's President Gustavo Diaz Ordaz met again in December, 1968 at the middle of the Santa Fe Street Bridge to formally mark settlement of the dispute involving several hundred acres of land. As part of the ceremony, water from the old bed of the Rio Grande was to be diverted to flow into a new concrete channel.

Television newscasters from both nations were on hand to record the great rush of water in the Rio Grande as it coursed into its new concrete bed separating the two countries. Since the Rio Grande has seldom been noted for its volume of water and is usually dry in December, and since the border communities didn't want the rest of the world to be disappointed, they stored up drainage water behind a small diversion dam (out of range of the cameras, of course). At a given signal, the flood gates were opened and the silvery Rio Grande flowed on cue; a beautiful stream of water came rushing down the concrete riverbed. Pictures were taken, hands were shaken, and within minutes the Rio Grande slowed to a trickle again.

The lengthy Chamizal dispute was the result of the meandering and flooding of the Rio Grande channel. According to the 1848 Treaty of Guadalupe Hidalgo, the Rio Grande was to

FRANKLIN CANAL for irrigation water from the Rio Grande used to flow between homes along Eighth Street in the Chamizal area of El Paso. The City covered and diverted the canal in the late 1960's as part of the redevelopment resulting from the rechanneling of the Rio Grande. The Paseo, as it is now called, is a safe, pleasant place for children to play.

be the boundary between the United States and Mexico. It sounded simple enough at the time. However, the river later changed its course and moved southward into Mexico. Americans moved into the vacuum on the theory that the center of the river was still the boundary. The Mexicans, understandably, did not see it that way, since the title to about 600 acres of thickly populated land was in question. The disputed area, once overgrown with chamizo, became known as the Chamizal Zone and was a sore spot in Mexican-American relations for a hundred years.

Since 1864, the administration of every American president attempted to reach a settlement. But it wasn't until the administration of John F. Kennedy that a settlement was made. The plan finally agreed upon was to build a new concrete channel for the Rio Grande through El Paso which ceded 630 acres of developed land to Mexico and transferred 193 acres of Mexican land to the United States. Mexico actually gained 437 acres by the transfer. About 100 acres of the far western end of the Chamizal was within the business district of El Paso.

More than 5,000 Americans living in the Chamizal had to be relocated to other parts of El Paso. They had to face the problems of moving to new neighborhoods and reestablishing businesses in new areas, but residents of El Paso and Juarez, long used to sharing in the life of both cities, accepted settlement as a means of opening older parts of their communities to new development.

ENGINE NO. 1 was built in 1857 and made its appearance in the Southwest in 1889. From 1909 to 1960 it reposed in a park at the rear of the Southern Pacific Building in El Paso. In 1960 the Southern Pacific Company gave the engine to El Paso Centennial Museum at U.T. El Paso.

WORKMEN move No. 1 up a special track to flatbed for the short journey to U.T. El Paso campus in 1960.

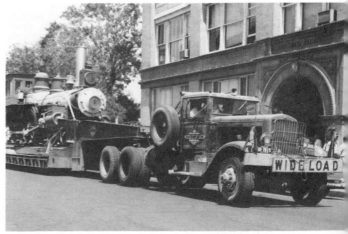

SAFELY LOADED aboard a trailer, No. 1 moves out. In the background is the Southern Pacific Building, now the American Bank of Commerce.

THE OLD El Paso High School building at Arizona and Campbell falls to the demolition hammer in the name of progress in 1964. It was known as Morehead School for almost a half century.

THE YSLETA DEPOT was retired from use and was awaiting demolition crews when this picture was taken in 1960.

PRESERVED FOR THE FUTURE is the charming old rooftop of the Ernest Krause
home built in the early 1880's. It now reposes with dignity on one of the shops in La Villita
shopping center. Below, the Trans-Mountain Road was completed in 1970
across the Franklin Mountains to provide easy access from the east to the west sides of El Paso.

EL PASO NATIONAL BANK's tower goes up, making a major skyline addition in 1962.
Note that the Hilton Hotel at right had still not been changed to the Plaza. Even the ornate
street lights had not yet been removed. Southwest National Bank Building (below)
and Downtowner Motor Inn gave El Paso a whole new look in 1964.

Old signs never die; they just fade in El Paso sunshine

COCA COLA sign on the Beckman Building, built in 1906, shows signs of wear and building modifications. Note the name "McClintock Co." which was the city's first major outdoor advertising firm.

THESE SIGNS, across from the Union Depot, are still there today and doing admirably well after more than a half-century in El Paso's bright sun.

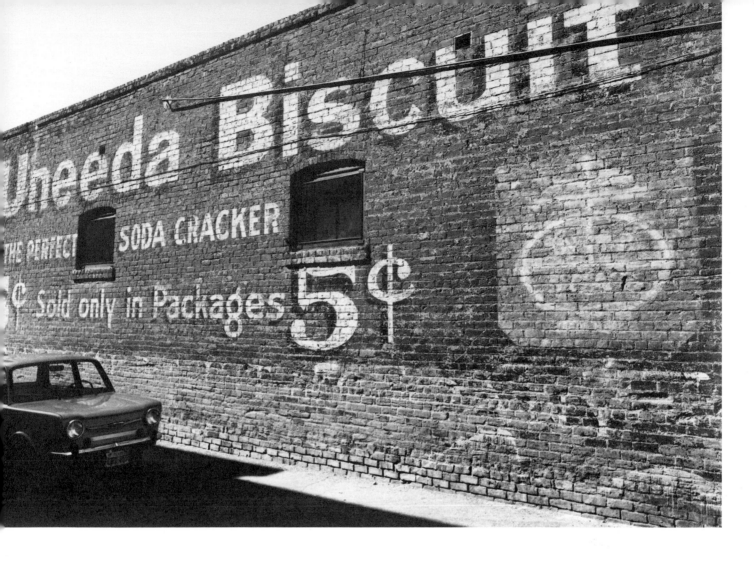

UNEEDA BISCUIT, as well as Coca Cola, was a big outdoor advertiser in the days when you could still buy crackers for a nickel. This sign is in the alley behind the El Paso Natural Gas Building.

"PLAN AHEAD" might be good advice for the modern-day sign painter who wrapped this sign around the building near the corner of Virginia and Overland.

Juarez: a new image and it still swings

AT JUAREZ RACE TRACK horses run during the afternoons and greyhounds race at night in season.

INTERNATIONAL STREETCAR, one of only six in the world, offers riders a tour of two cities in two nations. The trolleys make 630 trips a day between El Paso and Juarez.

WROUGHT IRON Volkswagen promotes the
unusual handwork done by talented Juarez craftmen.

CULTURAL MUSEUM in Juarez Pronaf
(Programa Nacional Fronterizo) area offers visitors
a look at pre-Columbian artifacts. The
Franciscan padre carved from wood (below) is
on display at the Arts and Crafts Center across from
the museum.

SUNDAY BULLFIGHTS still entertain fans
from both sides of the border.

STRIKING MEXICAN ARCHITECTURE
invites visitors to the Cultural Museum in Juarez.

163

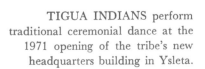

NEW LIFE STYLE for many El Pasoans is shown in this aerial photograph taken in 1971 with fourteen backyard swimming pools in an Eastridge neighborhood.

TIGUA INDIANS perform traditional ceremonial dance at the 1971 opening of the tribe's new headquarters building in Ysleta.

164

STATE NATIONAL BANK tower rises 22 stories.
Built in 1971, the State National now
occupies the site of the old Bassett Lumber Company.

NATIONAL advertisers
now realize what El
Pasoans have
known all along.

17-STORY HOLIDAY INN in the downtown
area changed El Paso's skyline in 1970.

NEW EL PASO INTERNATIONAL Airport
surrounds the old terminal building at left center of
this picture taken in 1971.

THE ONCE-EMPTY PASS that the Spaniards saw over 400 years ago has become two vital cities, El Paso and Juarez.

The Rio Grande forms the International boundary.

It is only fair to say that down through the years El Paso was, first of all, an oasis in the desert. You couldn't even call it a jumping-off place, because when you got to El Paso you were probably half-way there. For countless centuries this pass in the mountains and its river crossing was a pivotal spot for migrating Indians. For the Spaniards and the Mexicans and the Americans that followed, the oasis of El Paso provided food and water and shade and a place to rest before moving on.

Even by the middle of the 20th Century El Paso was not a place people went *to*. They usually went *through* — on their way to somewhere else.

Now it has grown up. It is no longer just a temporary stopping place to gas up on the way to California or the East. It is a place to live and work and bring up the kids in an outdoor, easy-living kind of way. The city has a symphony orchestra, a lively art museum, a mushrooming university. Its citizens have learned how to do more than just cope with the desert; they make it work for them. They have finally built homes with a style that belongs in this sunny, sandy part of the world. With irrigation they have turned a lot of it green. Half Mexican and half Texan, El Paso has put it all together. It has even developed a life style all its own.

And it still has Juarez across the river.

ACKNOWLEDGMENTS

It would be impossible to put together a book of this kind without the assistance and encouragement of literally dozens of people.

Like the El Paso Public Library, whose Lisabeth Lovelace, Glennis Hinshaw and Shirley Watson opened their hearts and the picture files of the wonderful Aultman Collection to me.

Like Cliff Trussell, Cletis Reaves and Bob Pinchback whose photographic talents are unequaled.

Like the artists: Fred Carter, Tom Lea, Jose Cisneros, Russell Waterhouse, John Paul Jones and Reynold Brown whose drawings and paintings made it possible to cover the whole canvas of El Paso history.

Like Millard McKinney who gave so much of his time and several of his most valuable pictures to make this book as accurate as possible.

Like the historians: Chris Fox, Cleofas Calleros, C. L. Sonnichsen and Leon Metz.

Like *The El Paso Times* and the *El Paso Herald-Post*

for opening up their files to me just for the asking.

Like Jonell Haley who spent many hours typing the manuscript and proofreading the galleys. And Martha Peterson, Lesley Gosling, Marta Lowe, Trudy Cottler and Marty LeVeck.

Like Jim Collins, a fine writer by profession, for reading the manuscript and making valuable suggestions.

Like Nestor Valencia and others at El Paso's City Planning Department; Elizabeth Snoddy, Ivan Hall, Raul Gonzalez and William Pearson.

Like all the people at Guynes Printing Company who had the faith and the know-how to produce this book.

Like Mike Brumbelow who insisted all along that this book should be done.

And above all, like my wife, Judy, whose great humor, enthusiasm and encouragement meant everything in bringing this book and its wonderful pictures to the light of day.

Interviews

Acosta, Trini
Alvarez, Baltazar
Bailey, Fred
Calleros, Cleofas
Casteel, Wylie and Kathren
Chambers, William
Collins, William
Decker, Hubert
de la Parra, Joe
Diaz, James
Dutton, Lyman
Finney, Robert
Fox, Chris
Gerald, Rex
Goodman, Eleanor

Hinshaw, Glennis
Hugg, Harlan
James, Elmer
Jaquez, Pete
Lovelace, Lisabeth
McFall, John
McKean, Mac and Hattie
McKee, Dave
McKinney, Millard
Mangan, Judy
Mangan, Peggy and Pancho
Mayfield, William
Metz, Leon
Miller, Richard
Montoya, Jesus

Morrow, Herb
Newman, Bud
Nix, Eddie
Oliver, Jodie
Patterson, Robert
Perrenot, Jane Burges
Richeson, Margie
Rister, Terry
Schwartz, Edward
Timmons, William L.
Valencia, Nestor
Walker, Dale
Waterhouse, Russell
Zabriskie, Mandy and Jean
Zwick, Fred

Picture and Art Credits

Jacket—Fred Carter

8, 9—Reynold Brown

11—Bob Pinchback from coin owned by William Timmons

12—British Museum and Nestor Valencia

13—Cliff Trussell and El Paso Centennial Museum

14—Jose Cisneros

15—Tom Lea

16—Top, Cliff Trussell and El Paso Centennial Museum; bottom Russell Waterhouse

17—Aultman Collection, El Paso Public Library

18—Top, *The El Paso Times;* bottom, Fort Bliss Information Office.

19—Top and bottom, Aultman Collection, El Paso Public Library; center, Cleofas Calleros Archives

20—John Paul Jones

20, 21—El Paso Public Library

22, 23—mgm Collection

24, 25—U.T. El Paso Archives

26—Top, El Paso Chamber of Commerce; bottom, Aultman Collection, El Paso Public Library

27—Top, *Harper's Monthly;* bottom, State National Bank

28—Top, Aultman Collection, El Paso Public Library; bottom, Leon Metz Collection

29—Top, Leon Metz Collection; bottom, Leon Metz Collection

30—Top, Frank Mangan Collection; bottom, El Paso Chamber of Commerce

31—Top left, Aultman Collection, El Paso Public Library; top right, Cliff Trussell and El Paso Centennial Museum; bottom left, Hudson-Fillmore Collection, El Paso Public Library; bottom right, *The El Paso Times* Blumenthal Collection

32—Cleofas Calleros Archives

33—Top, Aultman Collection, El Paso Public Library; bottom, U.T. El Paso Archives

34—Top, U.T. El Paso Archives; center, Aultman Collection, El Paso Public Library; bottom, U.T. El Paso Archives

35—Top, Otis Coles; bottom, Cleofas Calleros Archives

36—Top, mgm Collection; bottom, Cleofas Calleros Archives

37—Top, U.T. El Paso Archives; bottom, Aultman Collection, El Paso Public Library

38—Aultman Collection, El Paso Public Library

41—Top, mgm Collection; bottom, Aultman Collection, El Paso Public Library

42—Aultman Collection, El Paso Public Library

43—Top, Aultman Collection, El Paso Public Library; bottom, El Paso Electric Company

44—Aultman Collection, El Paso Public Library

45—Left, Aultman Collection, El Paso Public Library; top right, White House Department Store; bottom right, Eleanor Goodman

46, 47—Aultman Collection, El Paso Public Library

48—Top, Aultman Collection, El Paso Public Library; bottom left and right, Leon Metz Collection

49—Top, Aultman Collection, El Paso Public Library; bottom, Leon Metz Collection

50—Aultman Collection, El Paso Public Library

51—Top, Blumenthal Collection, *The El Paso Times;* bottom, Aultman Collection, El Paso Public Library

52—Top, Aultman Collection, El Paso Public Library; bottom, Mr. and Mrs. Bill Mueller

53—Top, Jack Vowell; bottom left, Aultman Collection, El Paso Public Library; bottom right, Cleofas Calleros Archives

54—Aultman Collection, El Paso Public Library

55—Top, El Paso Electric Company; bottom, Aultman Collection, El Paso Public Library

56—Aultman Collection, El Paso Public Library

57—Top, Aultman Collection, El Paso Public Library; bottom, Eleanor Goodman

58, 59—J. E. Morgan Collection, U.T. El Paso Archives

61—Top, Aultman Collection, El Paso Public Library; bottom, The White House Department Store

62, 63—Aultman Collection, El Paso Public Library

64—Top, The White House Department Store; bottom, The Popular Dry Goods Company

65—Aultman Collection, El Paso Public Library

66—Top, Aultman Collection, El Paso Public Library; bottom, J. E. Morgan Collection, U.T. El Paso Archives

67—*The El Paso Times*

68—Aultman Collection, El Paso Public Library

69—Top, Aultman Collection, El Paso Public Library; bottom Mr. and Mrs. Mike Brumbelow

SOURCES

Books and Articles

Binion, Charles H., *An Introduction to El Paso's Scenic and Historic Landmarks.* El Paso: Texas Western Press, 1970.

Broaddus, J. Morgan, *The Legal Heritage of El Paso.* El Paso: Texas Western Press, 1963.

Calleros, Cleofas, *El Paso Then and Now.* El Paso: American Printing Company, 1954.
El Paso's Missions and Indians. El Paso: McMath Co., 1953.

de Wetter, Mardee Belding. *Revolutionary El Paso: 1910-1917.* El Paso Historical Society, 1958.

Eckhart, George B., *Spanish Missions of Texas,* Arizona Archaeological and Historical Society, 1967.

El Paso *Herald-Post.*

El Paso *Times,* The.

Fugate, Francis L., *Frontier College.* El Paso: Texas Western Press, 1964.

Lea, Tom, *Twelve Travelers.* El Paso: Carl Hertzog, 1947.

Lee, Robert W., *An Illustrated History of El Paso. An Illustrated History of Fort Bliss.* Reprinted from El Paso *Herald-Post.*

McKinney, M. G. and C. L. Sonnichsen, *The State National.* El Paso: Texas Western Press, 1971.

McMaster, Richard K., *Musket, Saber, and Missile.* El Paso: Complete Printing and Letter Service, 1962.

Metz, Leon Claire, *John Selman, Texas Gunfighter.* New York: Hastings House, 1966.

Middagh, John, *Frontier Newspaper: The El Paso Times.* El Paso: Texas Western Press, 1958.

Mullen, Robert N., *Who Killed Pat Garrett — And Why?* El Paso: El Paso County Historical Society, 1971.

Neal, Dorothy Jensen, *The Cloud-Climbing Railroad.* Alamogordo: Alamogordo Printing Co., 1966.

Parrish, Joe, *Coffins, Cactus and Cowboys.* El Paso: Superior Publishing Co., 1964.

Sonnichsen, C. L. and M. G. McKinney, *The State National.* El Paso: Texas Western Press, 1971.

Sonnichsen, C. L., *Pass of the North.* El Paso: Texas Western Press, 1968.

This Fabulous Century, Vol. 2 and Vol. 4. New York: Time-Life Books, 1969.

Thomas, Laura, *A Short History of Northeast El Paso. A Short History of Ysleta, Texas. A Short History of Northwest El Paso.* El Paso: Department of Planning, City of El Paso, 1966.

Thomas, Laura, and Edwin L. Lent, William H. Pearson, and Elizabeth Hastings, *A Short History of South El Paso.* El Paso: Department of Planning, City of El Paso, 1967.

INDEX

This Book

is lithographed by Guynes Printing Company, El Paso, Texas.

The type for the text is 11 point Baskerville. Headings are set in Helvetica. The paper is 80 pound Mountie Matte.

The binding is by El Paso Bookbindery.